"The poems or meditations are immediate yet profound. They express beautifully thoughts or feelings I have had and give me new insights into life."

—Carol Bergeson, social worker

"Some of the passages made me read them over again and all sorts of things flitted through my mind that intrigued me. I have been working on expanding my prayer time, and the quality of it, too, and I think this book will greatly enrich that project."

—Connie Gill, member St. Thomas WATCH Community

Praise for Father Gutl's ***The Dancing Prophet,*** *also published by Loyola Press*

"Without singling out any of my own personal favorites I would like to strongly recommend these meditations to every type of reader. These pages will make you think. They will stir in you new and living experiences. They will give you the joy of recognition."

—*Father John Powell, S.J., from the foreword to* The Dancing Prophet

"The best gift of the book is Truth. Truth inspires, enlightens, and invests life with a sense of reality. When Father Gutl turns to the experience of living and senses the Mystery of God present, his artistry crafts a home for life experience which protects and secures it in time. It is for the happy reader to crack open the protective covering of words and so find him/herself face to face with Truth."

—*Monsignor James F. Campbell, Vicar General and Chancellor, Diocese of Peoria*

"*The Dancing Prophet* is, without doubt, one of the most precious gifts I have ever received. I have found myself going back over the meditations again and again—unable, I'm afraid, to read just one meditation at a time."

—*Chris Page, teacher, Adult Education*

WHAT GIVES ME STRENGTH

WHAT GIVES ME STRENGTH

REFLECTIONS ON THE
BASIC PRAYERS AND TRUTHS OF
CHRISTIANITY

MARTIN GUTL

TRANSLATED BY
JOHN F. LALANDE II

Loyola
Press
Chicago

Loyola Press
3441 North Ashland Avenue
Chicago, Illinois 60657

Originally published as *Was mir Kraft gibt*
© 1983 Styria, Graz/Austria; 5th printing, 1992

Cover design by Frederick Falkenberg.
Interior design by Tammi Longsjo.

Library of Congress Cataloging-in-Publication Data

Gutl, Martin, 1942–1994
[Was mir Kraft gibt. English]
What gives me strength : reflections on the basic prayers and truths of Christianity / Martin Gutl ; translated by John F. Lalande II.
p. cm.
ISBN 0-8294-0861-4 (alk. paper)
1. Catholic Church—Apologetic works—Popular works. 2. Catholic Church—Prayer-books and devotions—English. I. Title.
BX1754.G7713 1995
242—dc20 95-8781
CIP

It is easy to overlook the riches that God showers us with on an everyday basis, such as health, friends, and shelter—to name but a few. The basic prayers and truths of our Christian faith represent another example of such riches. Gutl's contribution in this work is to help us recapture the wondrous beauty and power of these priceless spiritual treasures. Through his meditations we come to view these basic prayers and truths as spiritual heirlooms that have been passed down lovingly from one generation of believers to the next.

This book invites all to a deeper understanding and appreciation of the most basic prayers and truths of our Christian faith. Those who accept the invitation will delight in the discoveries that await them.

—John F. Lalande II

About the Author

Father Martin Gutl was an Austrian diocesan priest and a remarkably successful writer of spiritual works. Before his untimely death in 1994 from a brain tumor at the young age of fifty-two, he had published more than a dozen books and become Austria's most beloved author of spiritual works. This book, a devotional work, has been a best-seller in Europe since its first printing; it will shortly undergo its sixth printing. His works have been translated into many languages, among them French, Italian, and Dutch.

While the Europeans have lost the ability to experience new books from this wonderfully gifted and insightful writer, we North Americans can rejoice in the fact that for us Gutl represents a new, vibrant voice, and one whose timeless works we are only beginning to savor.

CONTENTS

PREFACE

This book has grown from my desire to allow texts of faith, hope, and love to flow into one another.

Our profession of faith forms the foundation of our hope. Through hope we become capable of love. Countless encounters with people have made me realize how greatly we are threatened by doubt, dissatisfaction, negativism, condemnation, despair, and hate. Never before have people been offered such a vast array of life philosophies as today. Confusion and insecurity abound. Many people are in danger of viewing people and things from a one-sided perspective. To me, being Christian means taking up the Cross. It means living in the highly charged atmosphere between God's gift of grace and the human response to that grace. It means not striving to know God and humanity so that we might grow more powerful; rather, it means loving our neighbor and remaining humble in the process.

Always thinking we know better, always seeking to create our own way, our own recipe for being Christian, will not save us; it will only lead to bitterness and hardness of heart.

It is not a coincidence that Jesus Christ died for us on the vertical and horizontal beams of the Cross. He saved us where surrender and knowledge, truth and love intersect.

Today's world tempts us to suggest radical solutions as remedies for the crises that affect all aspects of life. Some struggle with spirituality, others with political reform. Some swear by the power of prayer, others are content with love of neighbor.

It is time we learned to bear the tensions inherent in the Cross, not change them.

Believers should ask themselves these questions: What are my hopes? What are the limits of my love? To greet people and to look at them with real love rather than indifference—that, in my opinion, represents a good start to being Christian.

To allow oneself, others, and God to remain a mystery despite all scientific inquiry is part of the challenge of love. We humans should not always categorize one another, but instead ask: Whom does the Creator will that I serve now? Our Christian faith leads us to introspection, to listen for what God wishes to tell us, to permit ourselves to grow and mature, to conquer and stand firm in the face of opposing views.

The texts in this book grow from my conviction that God will create goodness from everything that is within and without me. It is not for me to prescribe to Him the time required for such an undertaking.

My interpretation of the main prayers and basic truths of our Christian faith is based on the conviction that God loves each one of us. On the basis of this belief I see a part of God's plan in all suffering and joy, and believe that He desires our complete happiness.

This book is a book of faith. It is written because I have a special place in my heart for those in need of spiritual strength. May readers carefully heed not only its words, but listen to those of the Holy Spirit. This book is not about words or letters, but about the *Spirit* and *surrender.*

PRAYER IS POWER:

Meditations on the Basic Prayers of Christianity

THE SIGN OF THE CROSS

We point with an arm to on high.
From on high a precious,
positive flow of energy rushes toward us.
We point to on high,
not only to down below,
not only to the ground,
where worry, anger, and rage press us down.
The first thing we do in the morning is point
to on high,
to God, and say: "In the name of God."

I begin in the name of the Almighty,
not in the name of the unmighty.
In the name of God,
not in the name of a political party,
not in the name of a tyrant,
not in the name of a world hero,
not in the name of profit,
not in the name of a political campaign.
Not in the name of creed or church,
but in the name of God,
who looks down lovingly upon us as a father.

And so it is in the name of the Father,
in the name of a father,
not in the name of a law,

not in the name of an infinite machine,
but in the name of a loving You,
who is divine and human,
that I begin my day.

THE LORD'S PRAYER

Our Father

Who is for us?
Who is against us?
There was One who held us in His thoughts
long before it was possible for us to think of Him.
He gave us the opportunity
to grow and develop in this world.
In the beginning of the world
was God
not a coincidence!
A God,
a personal God,
not a law,
a YOU!
Jesus speaks of the Father.
Back then it sounded like blasphemy
to address God in a manner so tender, so intimate.

Let us build a relationship
with God, the Father,
during the course of our lives.
Let us pray in good times and in bad.
How incredible that prayer can become a home!
Instead of cursing
and wishing everything were damned,

let us pray the Our Father!
Instead of brooding and getting burnt out,
let us pause,
pray slowly, and with fervor
Our Father!

In heaven

Our Father in heaven.
Our Father in light.
Our Father when all is done.
We are on our way.
Father in heaven,
ahead of us all.
Father in us, with us.
Father in heaven.
Where You are, is heaven, happiness, and peace.
Where You are, is fullness of life.
Where You are, is home.
Where You are, is meaning.
Where You are, my questions grow silent.

Our Father in heaven.

Hallowed be Your name

We suffer from a desire for glory.
We overlook the source.
Hallowed be Your name!

Our tiny egos, fearful of suffering, must die,
die like a grain of wheat,
for in dying You will live in us.
Hallowed be Your name!

We need You
as our counselor from within.
Without You we are trapped
within our own thoughts.
We need humility
that You might teach us
the tenets of a life lived in wisdom.
In You we can come to full knowledge of who we are.
Hallowed be Your name!

We often overestimate ourselves
and suffer the consequences of pride.
We refuse to accept the idea
that without You we
are like trees without roots.
Hallowed be Your name!

Take away our pride!
Then we will be able
to accept gift after gift from You.
Your name will be hallowed
as we allow You to be God.
We do not pray to a stone,
but to a being
who is love.
Why do we withhold our trust?
There is a God
who hears us, understands and is able to help us
like no one else in the universe.
Why do we not pray with complete surrender:
Our Father?

Your kingdom come

Your kingdom come!
Great words of the mighty—
And the result?
New burdens, new constraints,
new rights for those in power.

Your kingdom come!
His kingdom is not forced upon us,
is not placed upon us like headgear.
It is built up by people.
With each good word
we say to one another,
His kingdom is enlarged.

With every prayer
we say,
His kingdom expands.
With every selfless act,
His kingdom grows.
His kingdom, where people are individuals,
not mere numbers or objects!

Your kingdom come!
Waiting and doing nothing
until God works the miracle;
making half-hearted efforts,
not trusting in grace:

both wrong attitudes
delay the coming of the kingdom!
We need neither revolution nor complacency!
Whenever HE can be in us,
HE will rule us.

Your kingdom come
with You
through us!

Your will be done

What has happened thus far?
Was everything Your will?
Who are You?

John answers:
God is love!
So why do we fear the request:
"Your will be done?"
We wince.
We think of pain,
of suffering, of sickness, and of death.
Your love be done!
How we understand love
is not always Your way of loving!

Your will be done!
Give us the courage to trust,
so that even life's most difficult hours
may become proof of Your love.
Give us the extraordinary peace of spirit
to wait, to become, to mature,
until we can say:
You willed it to be so.

Give us this day our daily bread

We admit
we need strength.
Our patience is quickly exhausted.
We had good intentions.
But nothing changed . . .

Give us our daily bread!
Bread we have,
it is love we lack.
Give us daily hope,
enthusiasm for everyday events.
Give us eyes
through which the events of everyday life
become an adventure.
Give us conversations
that help us on our way.
Give us people who come to us
and give us strength.
And send us to those
in need of our strength.

We have Sunday nourishment:
Eucharist, hymns, Communion.
But between Monday and Saturday
comes the long stretch
with the many run-ins
where we wear one another out!

We encounter someone
from another world:
Christ!

Give us our daily bread!
give us daily Spirit,
give us daily life,
give us Jesus, give us You!

Forgive us our trespasses

Forgive us
because we know not
what we do,
when we destroy the environment.

Forgive us our cowardice
in not keeping the promises
we have made.

Forgive us our insensitivities
in conversations with other people.
We listen, but do not to hear
what people wish to tell us.
We fail to hear the cry from the abyss.

Forgive us
for constantly making excuses
when the conversation involves giving.

Forgive us
for pointing to the words of sacred Scripture
as a blueprint for virtuous living,
yet failing to deal with the essence
of its challenges.

Forgive us
for having made

a harmless religious figure
out of Jesus.

Forgive us
for wanting to be faithful,
but not ready to change
our comfortable lifestyle.

Forgive us
for not wanting to assume
any responsibility for ourselves,
but instead assigning the blame
to forces beyond our control
like fate, politics, family fortunes, education.

Forgive us
for neither thinking for ourselves
nor for carrying out our own plans
out of fear
we might offend.

Forgive us
for using Your power
only so very sparingly!

Forgive us
our paralysis when we claim:
"There's nothing we can do!"

Forgive us our trespasses!
Open our eyes
that we might see
how much we could do in small ways!

As we forgive those who trespass against us

We can inflict great harm on one another.
The more we have trusted one another,
the deeper the pain of our disappointment.

We confess
that we have taken too little time
to examine ourselves.
And so what we know about other people
is likewise inadequate.
We become appalled
how a person we like
turns out:
different than we had imagined.
We become sad.

Forgiveness does not come easily.
The fact is, we are not angels,
but humans.
It takes a long time
for us to realize
that we too are to blame,
that we too are not superhumans.
We too have sinned,
either through too much understanding or too little.

We would like to forgive—
but despite all our thoughts on the matter

we hit against a wall
that separates us from one another.
When that happens a breakthrough must be attempted.
For that we need grace!
We can forgive
if You give us the strength to do so.

And lead us not into temptation

Lead us not into the abyss
where only darkness surrounds us,
where Your life-giving promises cannot be heard.
Lead us not to people
whose intelligent or stupid prattle
causes us to lose sight of our life's goals.
Lead us not to people
who ridicule our faith,
yet themselves are unhappy.
Lead us not to idols
who promise much,
yet will one day leave us nothing.

Protect us from hours
in which we begin
to cuss and swear.
Protect us from disappointments
we cannot endure.
You will test us
because we must learn to let go.
And since You do not deliver us
from challenges,
lead us when we are tempted.
Then all things
—even suffering—
will do us good!

But deliver us from evil

Deliver us from evil!
Deliver us from the pressure
of feeling we need to explain everything.
Deliver us from the overwhelming desire
to extract revenge
when a person hurts us.
Deliver us from the conceited view
that we must do everything ourselves.
Give us a mindset for partnership!
Deliver us from our pomposity!
Grant that we might recognize
other people's achievements!
Deliver us from the addictions
of wanting to be rich, respected, and important.
Help us
not to overlook those
who stand on the fringes of society,
who suffer,
who have failed, or who are sick.
Deliver us from evil
that suddenly befalls us!
Deliver us from addiction to power,
from blasphemy,
from bitterness,
from despair!
Deliver us from evil!

For Yours is the kingdom, the power, and the glory

Yours is the kingdom!
You are the fullness of being.
To You our prayers come.
In You are collected
all creation's songs of praise.
In You all human desires
flow together.
From You the Word went forth: Let there be light!
From You come the creative forces
that allow us to become, to grow, and to mature.
Your presence surrounds all worlds,
not only our earth.

Your kingdom encompasses all areas of existence.
To You we express gratitude for all things.
You we praise
because You are infinite, omnipotent Spirit.
You we glorify
because You never grow weary, never listless.
You we believe
because You came simple and poor
as Jesus of Nazareth.
We praise you
because Your kingdom will endure for us.
We glorify You
because our communion with You

will bring us eternal joy.
We thank You
because Your love is Your kingdom,
Your power, and Your glory!

THE MASS

We begin
the celebration of thanksgiving
with the Sign of the Cross,
with the name of the triune God.
We see ourselves for what we are
and ask for forgiveness.
We pray and listen and heed
what God has done with people
who before our time entrusted their lives to Him—
like Jacob and Abraham,
like Isaac, Moses, and the prophets,
like Jesus and the apostles.

We respond
with the Profession of Faith,
offer ourselves to God with bread and wine
at the Offertory.
Through this offering we become capable
of being free.
In this freedom we begin
to praise God in the Preface
and to thank Him.
We look to Jesus Christ
who gathers us together at the Lord's Supper
and says:
"Take and eat! This is my Body.

Take and drink! This is my Blood."
We pray the Our Father
and we receive the bread of life,
the Body of the Lord.

Jesus in us!
The light,
the peace,
the joy in us!
Now we shall radiate the light.
Now it is our turn to become bread,
offered up like Jesus!

Kyrie

To be allowed up.
Not stuck to the ground
with the false notion
that everyone
is spineless and apathetic.
To turn to God
when all attempts at self-improvement
have failed.
Kyrie eleison!

Lord, have mercy on us!
To be allowed to say "Lord,"
not just "Father"—Lord!
We need not only our
brothers and sisters,
fathers and mothers—
we also need the Lord,
whom we trust
will create in us order
out of chaos.

Kyrie eleison!
Where are our friends?
Why are all of you silent?

Why are all of you embarrassed?
Why do all of you act so cold?
You are all weary, weak, petty—
people, people with limitations.
Kyrie eleison!

Kyrie eleison?
Those who are superhuman
were either never born
or they have died out.
We deal daily with people
who are capable of anything:
from murder by means of words or a look,
to complete self-surrender.

Kyrie eleison!
To be allowed to pray,
not having to listen to
explanations for what's important and what's not!
To be allowed to pray!

Kyrie eleison!
Not just organizing,
studying, analyzing!
To be allowed to pray!
Kyrie eleison!

Shocking to be able to pray
in a world where everything has become doable.
In a world where science is triumphant,
to be able to pray.
  Lord, have mercy!
  Christ, have mercy!
  Lord, have mercy!

Gloria

Look not only down upon the earth—
Gloria in excelsis Deo!
Look up to the heavens!
Do not cling to the things of the world
as if possessed!
Here things quickly become too small,
too insufficient,
Here one finds anger, strife—
here earth becomes a grave, a prison,
a battlefield.

Gloria in excelsis!
Look up
without losing touch
with earthly realities.
Think about the role providence plays in life,
remember the stories of believers.
Gloria in excelsis!
Do not always look critically on creation,
or on your life!
Give thanks for being able to grow and develop,
that God and all of us exist!
Gloria in excelsis!

Before the Gospel

A word awaits you —
listen for it!
You have heard the texts of sacred Scripture
a thousand times before.
Everyday you are spoiled by new thrills.
Cast out your nets today!
You haven't caught anything,
you are bored.
You let the words
go right through you.
You already know everything by heart.
And yet a word, a sentence, a syllable,
or the pause between sentences
waits
for you.
Listen for it again!
God Himself
has a word just for you —
Listen here! Listen now!
If you listen attentively and with complete trust,
then the word that is on its way to you
will be able to arrive within you.

Offertory

How much have you given?
How much have you kept?
It is time now for your gift—
Don't lock yourself up! Open yourself!
Don't run off with your thoughts!
Stay here . . . and tell me:
What do you think of the people
celebrating Mass with you now?

You judge them by the way you look at them.
You've already classified them
as hypocrites, wimps, sickly types . . .
Preparation of the Gifts, Offertory, Sacrifice!
Offer up your classifications!
Love the people who are there
to the left and the right of you!
Begin with your own disarmament—
lay down your weapon!
Pray, surrender yourself to God!
Do not fear Him!
He has a plan for you,
which you in all your wisdom
could never have devised!
Offertory!
Go ahead and break the safety nets—
You will fall into God's hands.

Offertory—
Surrender yourself to Him
who loves you more
than you can ever love yourself!

Consecration

Ever since He said:
"Take and eat!
This is my body.
Here, take and drink!
This is my blood,"
He has been received
a thousand times over;
millions have
united with Him,
with the witness to the truth.
Suddenly they were
in the thick of the battle against falsehood.
They could feel the challenge:
Do not just receive this holy bread,
become bread yourselves!

With Him our lives are transformed.
Where once stress and strain were felt,
now His strength prevails!
Where once one question gave rise to another,
now songs of praise,
prayers of gratitude, and hallelujas are raised!

Ever since He said:
"Here, take and eat!
This is my body,"
we can no longer live selfishly,

with our own interests at heart.
From now on, being human means
receiving and offering oneself up.

Agnus Dei

A lamb that is being slaughtered!
We think of lions
as symbols of earthly power,
represented in many places.

Behold the Lamb of God!
What kind of goal is that?
To become a lamb
led to slaughter!
To be sacrificed—and then what?
Resurrection, life, fulfillment . . .

Agnus Dei—
You take away the sins of the world!
Not the one with power,
the One sacrificed takes away
the sins of the world!

Agnus Dei—
For centuries battles have raged,
deaths have occurred in the name of earthly powers.
The victors have basked in glory.

Behold the Lamb of God!
He shows us another way:
Being present, nonviolent, and good.
Behold the Crucified One,

the Resurrected One,
Jesus Christ,
God's way
of human redemption!

Dismissal

Do not go forth
without the peace of Christ!

Do not go forth
without thanking God from deep within
that He is your Father!

Do not go forth
without letting yourself be filled
with the Spirit of Strength and Love!

Do not go forth
without entrusting yourself
to God's care!

Do not go forth
without giving God a chance
to speak with you!

Do not go forth
without resolving
to be bread
for people
who need you!

Do not go forth
without having prayed
for your enemies!

Do not go forth
without letting yourself
be embraced by God!

THE PROFESSION OF FAITH

I believe

I believe.
I trust.
I open up.
I answer the question
that God puts to me:
"Where are you?"
I say: "Here I am!"
I let God touch me.
I believe.
I say to One
whom I do not see but sense
is the essence of all things,
I say: "You!"

I believe.
Faith reaches beyond knowledge.
Faith empowers me
to shape that which has not yet found form.
I believe.
I draw strength from the assurance
there is meaning, love, God.
I believe.

I sense
that in the sciences
we have captured
only a minute portion of reality.
My experiences
are a product of faith.

I believe in God

I do not believe
in something extinct.
I believe in something alive.
I believe in God.
I believe in a God
who walks with me.

I believe
in an infinite, eternal spirit,
not visible,
yet more powerful
than any visible force of the world.

I do not believe
in a figment of the imagination,
in an illusion,
but in an eternal,
living YOU.

I believe in God
not in ghosts.
I believe in God
not in a stubborn,
unbending, unimaginative, inept idol.

I believe in God
whose work can be witnessed.
I believe God
loves
each of us four billion human beings.

I believe in the infinite, compassionate God,
who waits for us as the Almighty
until we open ourselves to Him.
I believe in God
and believe
that with His help I can become human.

I believe in God, the Father, the Almighty

Many people have experienced miracles.
They prayed
that their sick mother might regain health,
and she became healthy.
Others prayed
that their gravely ill brother might be cured,
and he died.

Whether prayers are answered or not—
the mystery remains.
It is not for us to determine
when You, O God, intercede,
and when we must capitulate
to the laws of nature.

I believe in God, the Father, the Almighty!
It is important to remember that
there were miracles,
there are miracles today,
and there will be more tomorrow.

I believe in God, the Father, the Almighty!
I believe that You are almighty in us,
when we unite ourselves with You.
And I believe also in Your powerlessness
to change people
when they are unwilling.

I believe in the Creator of heaven and earth

I believe
in a creating God.

I believe
in becoming,
in a slow, gradual process of development.

I believe
in freedom,
in a free Creator.

I believe
that we are only at the beginning
of creation.

I believe
that inherent in all creation
is the drive toward completion.

I believe
that the process of slow, gradual development
in creation
is God's will.

I believe
that we humans receive
a share in God's consciousness

through faith,
hope,
and love.

I believe in God,
who allows freedom and necessity
to work together
in the gradual development of things and of humans.

I believe in Jesus Christ, His only begotten Son

I believe in Jesus,
Son of God,
because he was human—
human at every moment
and yet one with God.

We can derive infinite satisfaction from
the knowledge
that in Jesus we see the origin
of all humanity.
"Whoever sees me, sees the Father!"

With us Jesus prays
the Our Father.

I believe in the abandoned Jesus on the cross,
who in spite of everything found refuge in God.
I believe in the trembling Jesus on the Mount
of Olives,
who knew the Father would carry Him through.
I believe in the human Jesus,
in whom God was able to reveal Himself
as in no other human being.

I believe in Jesus Christ
because for me His example
gives Him credibility.

I believe
that through the Son of Man, Jesus Christ,
people have received a new yardstick
by which to measure humanity.

I believe
that Jesus Christ remains a witness to love
and to truth.

Born of the Virgin Mary

I know
whom to believe.

Born of the Virgin Mary.
She is centered totally on God.
She is not the property of any person.
Born of the Virgin Mary,
who lived in silence
that she might hear
the message of a quiet angel.

Born of a woman
who was able to be awed.

Born of a person
who trusted completely in God.

He came to us
as the poor man of Nazareth,
as the craftsman,
as the teacher and prophet,
as the One abandoned on the cross,
as the One who rose from the dead.

We thank you
for being able to entrust our lives
to this Jesus.

We thank you
that in this Jesus
we were able to discover
our own identity.

We thank you
that through this Jesus
the (hi)story of humans
became the (hi)story of God.

Suffered under Pontius Pilate

Many people lie under the cross,
crushed
by the weight of responsibilities.
Bent
by encounters with the unfortunate
they were unable to help.

Crushed
by the numerous questions
they were unable to answer.
Look at this one!
See how He suffers!
This man knows what it means to stumble,
to fall and collapse.
In His very appearance
He has become a cross.
Trunk and arms form a cross.

There are so many people who can't take any more!
They have grown weary of every path and detour.
Their strength is gone.
They are not sure
whether their prayers are being heard.

They have collapsed
under the burden of their own thoughts.
They have descended into hell.

They believe,
they hope,
even if they lie on the ground.
Even God bled,
lay under the cross,
had to be helped by Simon.

We see many
who have despaired,
people who have no one.
We are shaken
by the extent of suffering.

People lying on the ground
yearn
to be lifted up,
to be able to continue on,
and to be able to be strong.
I believe in Jesus Christ!

He knows what it means to feel human.
He says to us:
"I am with you,
even in the valley of death."

Was crucified, died, and was buried

Jesus Christ,
crucified, died, buried!

Jesus is not to be found among spectators,
nor among judges;
He is among those in history
who were crucified.

He did not philosophize
from a safe distance
on the interconnectedness of events in world history.
He came as a witness to the truth,
and as a witness to the truth
He was condemned and executed.

In view of the cross
one cannot help but ask:
Why did things have to be the way they were?
Why did a just man have to die?
Why did the witness to truth
have to be destroyed?

Why was there no reconciliation
between the Sanhedrin and Jesus?
Why did Jesus have to be crucified?

A look at the cross tells us
that terrible things happen in this world.

Help us
take seriously
the reality of this world
as a battleground
between truth and lies,
between good and evil.

On the third day He rose again from the dead

On the third day He rose again from the dead.

To be dead—on the other side of life:
to have died.
To be abandoned.
To be betrayed.
To be incapable of expression.
To be imprisoned within oneself.
To be dead.

To radiate no warmth.
To be unable to focus.
To be dead.

To be unable to grow and develop.
To waste away, all the while knowing
about one's latent talents.
To be unable to help oneself.
To be dead.

To spout clichés.
Not to think for oneself.
To be dead.

On the third day He rose again from the dead.
He opened himself

and everything began to give him joy:
his life, his environment,
his responsibilities, his development,
his future.
Rose again from the dead:
He could smile at the smallest things,
could return good for evil.

Rose again from the dead:
He overcame
his apathy,
his callousness,
his indifference
and became human.

On the third day He rose again from the dead:
Therefore, what once seemed final is only temporary.
Therefore, what I see now is still insignificant.
Because He who was dead is risen.

It is life
that reigns supreme over the universe,
not death.

Ascended into heaven

I believe in Jesus Christ,
ascended into heaven.

The Ascension of Jesus . . . it means:
He did not flee from us.
He comes to us
in new, mysterious ways,
no longer visible
in His human form.

He comes to us
in the appearance of many
who need us,
and whom we serve.

Ascended into heaven,
entered into our hearts.
Ascended into heaven,
drew closer to us than ever before,
in our many encounters with people.

I believe
Jesus Christ is with us now.
Wherever we recognize Him
is Emmaus,
is heaven,
is eternity.

He sits at the right hand of God, from where He shall judge the living and the dead

Jesus sits at the right hand of God.
The time of concealment is past.

He sits at the right hand of God:
He now has full insight
into His almighty Father's wonderful plan.

On the Mount of Olives He still had to struggle:
Your will—my will!
Your plan be done!
Now God's plan is also His.

Jesus will judge people,
those who think
and those who don't.
The brilliant and the insipid,
those closed and those open.

He will judge
non-Christians and Christians.

I believe in the Holy Spirit

I believe in the Holy Spirit
The Spirit creates life.
The Spirit is the force
that keeps everything in motion.
Not the will, not the intellect, not the emotions.

In the beginning of the human race
was inspiration.
God breathed upon the clay
and man became man.
Inspiration is liberation
of matter through the Spirit.

I believe
that religions and faiths
will draw closer to one another.
I believe
in the resolution of conflicts.
I believe
that our world
will continue to develop.
I believe
that whenever we are humble,
the Spirit of God prays within us.
I believe
that whenever we love
we speak the words of God.

Because the Spirit is love
and love is Spirit.

I believe in love.
I believe in the Holy Spirit!

I believe in the holy, catholic church

I believe in a universal church.
I believe that in future times
there will be
no more divisions, no more different churches.
There will be different forms of expression,
but only *one* religious consciousness.
I believe in a vast community of people
who are born in the Spirit,
and who through their life experiences
have found faith.
Life speaks but *one* language,
there can only be *one* truth.
I believe in the universal and holy
catholic church.

I believe that the current structure
of the church will change.
I believe that the church
will escape its influence.
And I believe that the Spirit of God
will prevail in the church.
I believe that we will overcome
the great ethnic divisions,
the great racial conflicts.
I believe that the church will be the elemental force
that brings people together.

I believe in a bridge
between this world and the next.
I believe that people
who have passed through death's door
will enjoy close relationships
with those still living on the earth.
I believe in the communion of saints.
I believe in the communion of the perfected
but also in the communion
of the imperfect.
I believe in the communion of seekers.
I do not believe
that the meaning of this world, the meaning
of humankind,
which has evolved over millions of years
into its present form,
can be death.
I believe
in the resurrection of the dead.

I believe in the communion of saints

I believe that there are people
who are complete.
They have traveled a long path
to maturity.
They, the complete ones,
wait for us to speak to them.
I believe in a community of helpers
in heaven and on earth.

I believe that people who trust
live in an atmosphere
in which the saints are near.
I believe in messages from the saints.
I believe in a community of saints.
I believe that we can become holy.

We believe that the saints
have attained their goal.
They remained kind
in a world of hate,
they remained truthful
in a world of lies;
above all they trusted,
even though Your protective hand
could not be seen with the naked eye.

They believed
when others doubted.
We thank You for these people
who served as outlets for Your power.

I believe in the forgiveness of sins

I believe that we commit sin
because we are free.
I believe in human freedom.
I believe that we possess the potential
to do one another good and to harm one another.
I believe that we can either recognize ourselves
for who we are
or live a life of self-deception.

I also believe in the forgiveness of sins.
I believe that our repentance of sin
teaches us an important lesson.
I believe in the teaching of Jesus
that the one who is forgiven more
will also love more.

I believe in the resurrection of the dead

I believe in daily resurrection.
I believe that those who despair
can be changed
through confident assurances.
I believe that the narrow-minded
will be able to attain broadened intellectual
perspectives.
I believe that the greedy
will be able to recognize the error of their ways
and begin to give without fear.
I believe that someday
the forces of good will prevail.
I believe that humanity,
through the power of the spirit,
will be able to preserve the health of the body.
I believe that the sad,
through an encounter with a Simon
who can show them a way of life built on faith,
will be able to find happiness.
I believe that religions
and faiths will unite.
I believe that despite numerous crises
this world will move toward goodness.
I believe in meaningful development
of human resources.
I believe that God, not a coincidence,
created the world.

I believe that God gives us an infinite amount
of freedom
to shape our own lives.
I believe that we must take our fate
into our own hands.
I believe in the resurrection of the dead.
I believe that there is no end for us,
only another fresh start
with a new view and with dedication.
I believe in the value of self-surrender,
in the transformational power of love
that never grows bitter from negative experiences.
I believe.
I trust
that God will be able to make all of us happy.
I believe in the Resurrection!
I shall open my hands
to receive His gifts.

I believe in life everlasting

We are here on earth
for a brief test.
I believe in life everlasting.
I believe
that everyone receives the opportunity
for eternal happiness.
I believe
that God has an infinite number of means at
His disposal
for allowing us to mature even beyond death.
I believe
that God loves us unconditionally
and will stop at nothing
to complete His work of creation in us.
He will do whatever is necessary
for us to attain our goal,
our holiness.

God is love.
Love will do everything in its power
to help us
attain our eternal happiness.
I believe
in eternal life,
in eternal joy,
in eternal friendship,
in God and in people.

THE HAIL MARY

Hail, Mary

Hail, Mary!
I, the angel of the Lord,
bring you greetings from the Most High.
He needs your trust.
God awaits your *yes!*

Rejoice, O human!
God's thoughts are turned to you.
He has singled you out
from among billions of humans.
He calls you by name!
God needs you!

Full of grace

You are full of grace!
Your life is one of fullness.
God will reveal to you
the riches of His ways.
What is His, is yours!

O human, you are filled
with good gifts,
you are full of potential
because the Lord is with you!

The Lord is with you

To be accompanied, to be surrounded
by divine protection.
Knowing that the Almighty
is at your side!

He is in you, with you,
beside you, over you.
You need never fear
being alone!
Your path has been made safe.
God has given you His angels.
The Lord is with you!

Blessed are you among women

You experienced
who God is
back in Nazareth,
back in Bethlehem,
back during the flight to Egypt,
back on Calvary,
back at Pentecost,
back when you were taken up
into heaven.

We need your experience, Mary!
You share it with us
in every Hail Mary.
In you we too are greeted,
singled out by God!

Blessed is the fruit of your womb

That which was created
is the fruit of adoration
and the fruit of surrender,
the fruit of trust.
The word *yes* bore fruit.
The one who believes will become holy.
The one who shares will receive.
The one who listens will receive wisdom.
The one who receives will be able to give.
Mary brings Jesus into the world.
The light has taken on human form.

Holy Mary, Mother of God

Through difficult and dark periods,
through moments that defied logical explanations,
you kept
your faith.
The questions you posed in grief
could not dim your spirits
or shatter your loving trust.

Pray for us sinners

Your intercession
quells our impatience.
We examine ourselves
yet know not
who we are.
Unable to wait,
we despair ourselves to death.
Help us to stop
and look deep within.
Pray for us restless sinners
that we too might offer the eternal Word
a home in us.

Now and at the hour of our death

Help us now
when our needs and the needs of others
confuse us;
now, when greed for profit,
when war and avarice
plague us;
now, when fear and superficiality
darken the clarity of our view.
Help us now
lest we lose our way.
Now and in the hour of our death!

At the hour of our death help us
to die in gratitude,
to pass away with our souls at full power
and nothing less.
Help us, holy Mother of God,
to die in love,
and humbly and joyfully in eternity
to present the Lord
with the harvest of our years on earth.
Help us now
and at the hour of our death!

THE ROSARY

A Way to Peace

To be at peace. Words, repeating prayers—with the recurring Hail Mary and the mystery of salvation embedded in those words, our restless spirit finds peace. Our thoughts, which shift abruptly from this to that, move toward hope. Our mood, which is subject to so many swings, becomes stable. An inner joy, a joy of knowing that there is a God, that there is love, begins to carry us. Thoughts begin to break up like clouds. Thoughts of hate and of anger give way. Understanding begins to grow. Our prayer becomes a source of strength.

Able to do without. To do without understanding individual words. To pray without wanting to understand the words, without wanting to know their deepest meaning. To pray like people before us prayed when they said the rosary en route to the cemetery, as they struggled to cope with the most difficult of all losses. To be able to pray, pray the rosary; to take leave of one's own importance while thinking of Mary. Mary the maiden. Mary as instrument. If we can surrender ourselves to God as Mary did, certain things will not seem so terribly important; we will not argue with malice over various things.

We will not be as concerned about changing the world as about taking on ourselves, transforming ourselves.

The prayer of the rosary—a meditative form of prayer, an opportunity for Christian meditation without big words; a form of renunciation whereby we surrender the need for logical explanations to everything. Through the mysteries of the joyful, sorrowful, and glorious rosaries we discover the path we must walk to becoming human.

To be on the Way. To approach people in trust, out of faith, at peace; to take our time, until an insight begins to form. To be able to surrender ourselves to God, and not persist stubbornly in realizing our own plans! To travel different paths, to search until we have rediscovered peace; to expose ourselves to human suffering until we ourselves are deeply moved. To be scourged by the words of those not following the way we go, but who ridicule us. To be crowned with thorns, with words that pierce our hearts, that agonize. To go the Way of the Cross, to walk a path, not run from it; to continue along that path until insight develops, until peace returns. To be crucified, able to die. To be made new, to be resurrected; to be resurrected from the dead by an eternal, magnificent force. To ascend into heaven; to experience heaven, a piece of heaven during a moment of prayer, of conversation with people, in the solitude of nature. To receive the Holy Spirit, to be moved by thoughts of God, to be seized by His thoughts, to be filled with His Spirit. To be taken up into heaven, to feel the embrace, the union with God. To be crowned! To recognize life as a mosaic in which every pebble was essential for the formation of a beauteous image. To see salvation history as a rainbow; Roman, Gothic, and Baroque arches as symbols of reconciliation and union. Yes, that is the path to becoming human, the path of every human.

The Joyful Mysteries

I. The Annunciation
(Jesus is conceived of the Holy Spirit)

Before you give, receive!
The One conceived by the Holy Spirit!
There is Mary, a human being—and there is God.
There is a plan.
God does not remain in heaven,
God goes to His people.
There is a girl.
She has many thoughts,
she has a burning desire
that she cannot describe.
She is quieter than other girls.
She is full of life.
When all is quiet she looks off into the distance.
She waits for someone.
The angel Gabriel stands before her!
On a mission from God involving a human.
You will conceive of the Holy Spirit!
You shall become the mother of Jesus.
How shall that happen?
You will receive.
Before you can give birth, you must receive
the mystery of life.
This person will be conceived and received,
He will be born.
Conceived by the Holy Spirit!

You did not cling stubbornly to your own dreams
of happiness.
To allow oneself to be led, to take one's time,
to become a holy instrument of God's plan.
To conceive of the Holy Spirit!
To allow the Holy Spirit
to control the course of one's life,
to become human, to open oneself
to God and His designs.

II. The Visitation
(Jesus is carried to Elizabeth)
Mary carries Jesus to Elizabeth,
trusting in the mystery
as she goes to another person.
One person with a recent experience of God
goes to another person
who has also been moved by God.

Mary and Elizabeth meet one another,
the one highly favored
and the one deeply moved!
With God nothing is impossible.
In the meeting of the two women
God is praised.
They marvel at the truth of the words:
"The Lord is with you!"
They are uplifted.
They see: in me, in you
our mysterious God is at work!

Waiting with one another for the miracle,
praying with one another—
that is church on a small scale.

Two believers approach one another
and discover themselves in God.
They experience the mystery of the intimate God
through the mystery of human intimacy.

They are filled with the certainty
that God is here,
that God is at work among us now.

Mary and Elizabeth,
two people
who let God in.

III. The Nativity
(Jesus is born in Bethlehem)

There's a woman and her husband,
both weary—the long journey
from Nazareth to Bethlehem.
She feels the child; it presses to enter the world.
What kind of world will this child enter?
Bethlehem—a place without love.
We have no room for you!
No place for those coming,
for the children!
Where shall I give birth?
You are supposed to become the mother of Jesus!
What now? Am I seeing things?
That place—a pitiful place(!)—
is becoming a temple, is becoming a home for God.
Mary and Joseph—
Mary gives birth—Jesus has arrived!
Nine months of long waiting,
hoping, trembling, praying, marveling.
Now he is here!
Jesus!
What history lies hidden within this Jesus?
Mary's gaze upon the child,
Joseph's gaze upon Jesus—
what will happen?
What has already happened?
The last few months
since the encounter with the angel—

how different life is
when we surrender our lives to God!
What happens then?
The circumstances—what kind of people
do we become?
Born in Bethlehem:
faith begins to take shape,
hope becomes visible.
The things we imagine in quiet,
the things that quietly mature within us
will someday take shape,
will become visible, apparent in our very midst
as attitude, as gestures, as life.

IV. The Presentation
(Jesus is presented in the temple)

There is a child.
Jesus.
How great the longing for Him!
And there is a mother.
Mary.
Her child—and not just her child.
She is aware of the mission:
Son of God!
This child is not hers to keep.
She enters the temple with her child
and in a symbolic gesture gives it to God.
The child is circumcised,
received
into the community of faithful Israelites;
initiated into the people of God,
into the family of those who trust in God,
who know: children belong
not only to their father and mother,
children belong to God.
He is the source of life.
To surrender oneself to God, to be thankful
means being able to sacrifice.
To give God a share in what is mine,
and to rejoice in being human.
To thank God for one's life!
Just as Abraham acted out of faith in surrendering
his son Isaac to God,

letting go of him in the hour of sacrifice,
and then receiving him back again as a new gift,
we too must be able to let go of all
we would rather keep.
Self surrender to God—
a way to find peace.

V. The Finding in the Temple
(Jesus is found in the temple)
There are Mary and Joseph.
They are looking for Jesus.
They are looking for Him everywhere.
Distressed they search for Him.
They have questions,
questions of God,
questions of Jesus
when they find Him.
"Didn't you know
that I had to be about
my Father's business?"
What kind of world is it
that Jesus lives in?
What kind of path is it
that Jesus walks?
Not one necessarily obedient
to His parents.
Didn't you know?
What kind of knowledge is that?
What kind of consciousness?
Rediscovery in the temple;
being wounded on earth
and sensing intuitively: healing occurs only
if I remain mindful of heaven.
Being wounded, losing peace
through hectic activity.
Wanting to be happy on earth.

What people won't do
to find happiness on earth!
And the result?
Broken spirits, disappointment.
Rediscovery in the temple!
Didn't you know
that there's more to life than
earning money,
worrying about your marriage?
Didn't you know
that there is a love
greater than any other?
Didn't you know
that I have to be about
my Father's business?
That I had to follow the voice within me
to find my peace?

The Sorrowful Mysteries

I. The Agony in the Garden
(Jesus sweat blood for us)

There is one person kneeling,
yet how many are there on earth?
There is one person who looks into the future.
He knows what lies deep within the human heart.
He worked miracles by trusting in God,
said to a dead Lazarus: "Come forth!"
and Lazarus came.
There is one person kneeling
who knows that the hour
of the prince of darkness has come;
the hour that He must suffer,
in which a new reality will begin.
He feels the pain,
His body breaking down.
He feels the abandonment—
and how His friends have gone into hiding;
how no one will stand by His side.
He feels how everything has changed.
It's one thing to say:
"Father, I praise You!"
It's another to say:
"If it is possible,
take this cup away!"
The One who sweat blood for us!

Like Him, many good people
have faced difficult situations.
Like Him, many tremble.
Like Him, there are many who suffer
because they stuck to their principles,
because they were true to their nature.
The One who sweat blood for us!
The ones who have sweat blood for us:
who remained witnesses to the truth
in the midst of masses
who live in untruth.

II. The Scourging at the Pillar
(Jesus was scourged for our sake)

To be scourged,
with looks and words;
to be scourged,
to be beaten.
And He was scourged for our sake!
There is one person
people judge,
people don't see,
people don't hear,
people talk about.
And He was scourged for our sake!
There is one person,
too good in the eyes of others,
an idealist.
People ridiculed Him.
There is one person
people can easily attack.
People can hit
and beat a person to death
with words and with silence,
can scourge in different ways!
There is a human being
who cannot defend himself,
who was never told:
Build a wall around yourself!
Protect yourself,
lest you fall prey to the lions!

There is a defenseless person.
People attack Him.
And He was scourged for our sake!
There is a victim of power.
Arguments count for nothing,
reason remains silent.
Violence and aggression attack, strike.
People have no arguments,
only fists.
And He was scourged for our sake!
One, not just one,
in the meantime many
have been beaten with Jesus,
treated unfairly.
All of them are an appeal:
Reconsider, think about what you are doing!
Are you one who joins in the beating,
if not, who are you?
Think about it!
What do you do
when judgments about others
are made in your presence?
And He was scourged for our sake!

III. The Crowning with Thorns
(Jesus was crowned with thorns)
There is One
who did not wish to become king.
He multiplied loaves of bread,
wanted to focus people's attention on another world.
People wanted Him to be a leader and ruler
in this world
because He could change stones into bread,
effortlessly make crowds
follow Him.
There is one person,
a radiant individual
who could transform.
There is one person
who in this world could achieve His goals
on the strength of His personality.
Yet he says:
"Blessed are the poor;
blessed are those who hunger;
blessed are the meek;
blessed are you when they persecute you."
They had to make this person
an object of ridicule.
He is crowned with thorns;
not with jewels,
with thorns He is crowned.
There is one person
made a laughingstock.

Because in this world
He did not succeed.
Crowned with thorns for our sake!
Like Him, many people have been ridiculed
because in the midst of this world
they believed in another world.
Because they built their fortunes not only
on this world,
but also on the other.
The ones who for our sake were crowned
with thorns,
with looks of skepticism,
with derisive comments.
The One—the many,
who because of their Christian commitment
have been crowned with thorns.

IV. The Carrying of the Cross
(For our sake Jesus bore that heavy cross)

One, who was permitted to experience the fullness
of joy,
who attained fullness of life,
fullness of consciousness;
One, who experienced the beauty
of the human soul.
One, who was able to experience the full magnititude
of a relationship with God;
One, who transformed people;
One who showed the path
that leads to love:
Now, with heavy beam, He walks the path
to Golgotha.
For our sake He bore that heavy cross!
We thought things would turn out differently.
Even He thought things might turn out differently!
Certainly a man with influence,
couldn't He convince
the Pharisees and Scribes,
the elders in the Sanhedrin?
Why did He have to walk this path?
Lonely, ostracized, He walks out
from Jerusalem,
to die before the city walls.
For our sake He bore the heavy cross!
Why is the world so different
from how we imagined it?

Why is everything so different
from how we planned it?
For our sake He bore the heavy cross!
There goes a person,
a person who was God and man;
a person who is one of us and of God.
There goes a person walking out
to die on the cross.
There are many who go out
to die an early death:
through sickness and natural calamities,
through accidents and famine.
There are many going out, who have bled to death
in war or elsewhere.
The ones who bore a heavy cross for our sake,
before us, for us.

V. The Crucifixion
(Jesus was crucified for our sake)

Golgotha!
There it is, the hill!
Outside the walls of Jerusalem,
between two criminals
His cross is mounted.
The stage is set for the Righteous One,
the stage of the Redeemer!
There He hangs, the One who is free,
nailed to the cross.
Beneath him John and Mary:
"Behold your son!
Behold your mother!"
Jesus dies on the cross.
Jesus lets go of everything,
even Mary and John;
He even lets go of the idea
that the Father might still help Him.
"Why have you abandoned me?"
Even that dies in Him,
that kind of faith.
A new faith is born:
"Father, into Your hands I commend my spirit!"
I stop thinking,
I stop creating images for myself,
of expecting something for myself.
I place myself into Your hands.
That is how Jesus dies.

The One who died on the cross for us!
How many have died in trust,
in despair, and then again in trust.
In abandonment and then in the security
of an omnipresent God.
The One who died on the cross for us!

The Glorious Mysteries

I. The Resurrection
(Jesus rose from the dead)
The drama on the cross,
it came to an end.
Death.
A new life begins.
Jesus is risen.
He took with Him into eternity
the experience of His earthly existence.
The marks of His wounds glow.
Through Him we have the assurance
that our eyes
see but a part of reality.
What did people see in Jesus Christ on the cross?
One who died.
People heard the cries of abandonment.

The Resurrection is not an event
for reporters and photographers.
Jesus came to those
who trusted in Him.
He did not reveal himself to doubters.

There were enough witnesses to the Resurrection.
One, who had himself been unsure and denied it,
became the rock
upon which the community of believers

could be built up.
Apostles once confused
became sources of hope.
People once poor
could make others rich.
People who themselves had suffered
now loved unconditionally.
People who had seen the Resurrected One alive
made it possible for His Resurrection to be seen
in their lives.

II. The Ascension
(Jesus ascended into heaven)

You continue to be angry,
you continue to be perturbed,
withdrawn,
bitter.
Read sacred Scripture!
Read about people like Abraham,
what he felt,
what he suffered,
what he had to endure!
How he had to wait
until Isaac was given to him.
Read about Moses!
About the long journey through the desert;
about the crises
that he experienced.
Read about the prophets,
how they were persecuted!
Read about Jesus,
what He went through!
Read about the first Christians,
what they experienced and suffered!
You will grow quiet.
You will free yourself
from your negative thoughts.
You will be grateful
and suddenly ascend into heaven,
suddenly experience a new state of being,

a state of union,
of security.
He ascended into heaven!

III. The Descent of the Holy Spirit
(Jesus sent us the Holy Spirit)

He sent us the Spirit.
Spirit—
as source of life,
as source of wisdom,
as source of peace.
All things are made of spirit.
Even matter is condensed spirit,
imprisoned spirit,
incarcerated spirit.
He sent us the Spirit!
Like a storm in the quiet,
he sent us the Spirit,
the force of love
in fiery tongues.
He sent us the Spirit!
A Spirit that helps us
ponder mysteries in silence,
to pass on what we know,
to build up communities
supported by the Spirit.
He sent us the Holy Spirit!
Not the spirit of being a know-it-all,
not the spirit of strife,
not the spirit of narrow-mindedness.
The Spirit of openness,
the Spirit of love,
the Spirit of peace.

IV. The Assumption
(Jesus took you, O Virgin Mary, up into heaven)

He embraced you in heaven.
You arrived in heaven
where there was One
who embraced you: God.
Soul, God waited for you!
Now you are one with him.
He embraces you.
You followed your calling.
You lived in accordance with His Word.
You became the answer to His Word.
Now you are home.
Now the questions are silenced.
Now you give thanks.
Now you sing: "Halleluja!"
Now you say: "Thanks be to God!"
Your journey is behind you,
the peaks, the valleys, the ravines.
Mary, rejoice!
Mary, shout for joy!
Because all that you believed in
has been fulfilled.

V. The Crowning of Mary
(Jesus crowned you,
O Virgin Mary, as Queen of Heaven)

Mary, crowned in heaven!
The moment has finally arrived.
The faultfinders are silenced,
the doubters are silenced.
Heaven is quiet.
You are being crowned.

You are a maidservant,
you were not a ruler!
You did not succeed
by elbowing your way ahead.
You did not want to be number one.
You had the courage,
the humility, to serve.
Now you are being crowned,
fantastic!

Hail, O human,
who had the courage
to serve in this world;
to not just ask "why,"
but to say "thank you";
to be second or third;
to sacrifice;
to suffer
and to renounce all things

until beauty would come to you
in this world
and in the next.
You are being crowned.

Halleluja!

THE ANGEL OF THE LORD
(Angelus)

Three levels of Christian thought and formation are indicated in this prayer: first, to be able to hear the Good News and receive it from the Holy Spirit; second, to recognize oneself as a servant of the Lord; and third, to let the Lord's will be done—to be aware that there is a plan greater than my own, that some One has a greater love than I—to let the Lord's will be done!

The Angel of the Lord declared unto Mary

There is a plan.
There is God
who sends an angel.
And there is a young girl
who keeps watch.
The angel of the Lord
could be seen by Mary
because she trusted.

The angel of the Lord
declared unto Mary.
So many angels are moving about,
and are not seen by us,
heard or noticed.
We let many angels pass us by!

The angel of the Lord—
he awaits us in many guises,
even in human guise,
in the guise of a flower,
in the guise of a tree,
in many, many guises.

And she conceived of the Holy Spirit

Yes, there is One
who sends a message.
But what unusual news:
"She conceived of the Holy Spirit!"
Mary waits,
the child grows within her.
She conceives of the Holy Spirit
because she sees more than what's visible to the eye,
she sees far beyond.

Mary said: Behold, I am the handmaid of the Lord

Mary does not ask:
Who am I?
What can I do?
What must I do
to be happy?
She believes in herself
as handmaid of the Lord.
She knows
she will only understand
if she serves.
She asks:
"How shall this happen?"
And she hears:
"With God, nothing is impossible."

Behold, I am the handmaid of the Lord!
Behold, I am a person
who listens,
who believes,
who trusts.
Behold, I am a person
who is here,
who prays,
I am a person
who is here when she is needed.
Behold, I am the handmaid of the Lord!

Be it done to me according to Your Word

Yes, be it done!
I don't have to understand everything.
I trust before I understand.
That's Mary. That's faith.
That's trust.
If things only happened
that we understood,
how little greatness
there would be in this world!
How many people were in a position to understand
from their experiences
what their mission was,
what they had to do!
How many people were in a position to understand
that their great suffering,
which totally consumed them,
and which allowed them to mature,
also endowed them with a new radiance?
Mary trusts
before she understands.
And greatness happens!
Be it done to me according to Your Word!

Mary refuses
to feel that she must do everything herself.
She simply says: "Be it done to me!"
It is done.

She is not passive.
She has enough to do.
She becomes a mother.
She was not spared that task,
even though she let it be done.
But in everything that happened
she knew:
God is present!
Whether in Bethlehem,
or forced out to the edge of town
and giving birth in isolation;
whether in flight to Egypt:
Mary was there!
Be it done to me according to Your Word!

And the Word became flesh and dwelt among us

Things progressed beyond the Word.
The Word became flesh.
It took on form,
entered our world.
The Word became flesh
and dwelt among us!
Whenever we trust, believe,
something concrete will happen:
A person suddenly regains health.
An embittered person suddenly becomes someone
we can talk to.
A person once despaired
is suddenly able to hope.
The Word became flesh!
Those who trust
will experience God in concrete ways.

THE JESUS PRAYER

Jesus, You I love; Jesus, for You I die;
Jesus, I am Yours in life and in death.

This prayer has given
strength and support
to countless numbers of people.
They have felt uplifted
and protected by this prayer.
This prayer has enabled them
to take part in the life of Jesus.
Christians need an ongoing dialogue
with their Lord and Master.
With each prayer of the heart
their union
with Jesus Christ can grow.
Lovers know the necessity
of constant communication.
It demands more than
words and eye contact.
It has more to do with
an inner disposition of "existing for the other person."
Our whole lives long we should
remain in conversation with Jesus.
To pray means to surrender oneself,
to trust in Jesus.

Then His Spirit assumes the leadership role
in my prayer.
We should give Jesus the opportunity
to work on us.
We want so much
to realize our own plans.
But Jesus Christ has greater plans
for our lives.
He should be our master.

THE GLORY BE TO THE FATHER

Glory be to the Father, and to the Son, and to the Holy Spirit

O human, realize your value!
God wishes to work through you.
You are important to Him!
Long before you were able to think of God,
He loved you.

But, human, do not overestimate yourself!
You have been given a command
to place yourself at God's disposal.
Therein lies the dignity of the human person,
that God wishes to work through that person.

Examine the history of humanity,
how people without God
tried to achieve their goals.
What was the result?
The oppression and ruin
of people.
The idea of life did not originate with us,
it is not we who created the universe.
Therefore it is necessary

to investigate
the secrets of the universe
with a spirit of humility and reverence.
Day and night
a triune God turns to us.
To Him be glory!
To Him do our body and soul belong.
We are not the owners of our lives.
God is that life.
Only when we praise Him
will we see ourselves in the right Spirit.
Glory be to the Father!
When we pray in this way
we guard ourselves against delusions of grandeur,
against vanity and a cold heart.

"Glory be to the Father . . . "
A prayer for the mighty of this world
and a prayer for the poor.
A political prayer
and a personal prayer.
It can save our human dignity
and help us to secure peace.

As it was in the beginning, is now, and will be forever

We have no other choice
but to think and measure things in time.
For God,
the border of past, present, and future
will never exist.
His thoughts are not always
our thoughts,
His ways not our ways.
He sees the world
and the development of humanity
differently than we.
For us, many things remain a mystery.
That which we experience momentarily
as little more than bad luck
we can later recognize
as necessary to the process of our development.
God has a clear view of our future and
its possibilities.
We should place ourselves in His trust and pray:
Glory be to the Father . . .

THE BODY AS MESSAGE:

Reflections on Bearing and Posture

People often bemoan the gap that separates intellect from feeling. In Christian churches there are prayers formed by the words and postures adopted by people praying. Over time, people have come to realize that body and soul are meant to work together, even in prayer. Various postures tell us something not only about one's outward bearing but also about one's inner disposition. Different postures evoke different feelings. Prayer is not just a matter of the mind. Human beings exist in their bodies, in their feelings, and in their thoughts. In the following texts I have attempted to reflect on the various positions of the body at prayer. Certain prayers are traditionally linked with certain postures. Prayers should lead to quiet, to peace. Posture and prayer work together. The result is harmony.

FOLDED HANDS

In folding my hands I profess
the polarity of my existence.
We are dealing with two hands,
not just one.
Folding two hands,
guiding them slowly toward one another.
How important it is in conversations
to recognize two poles of reality.
We have resistance that is justified
and surrender that is necessary.
Grace and human endeavor,
God's gift and people's surrender,
trust and control.
Things one-sided are flawed
because God created heaven and earth,
man and woman,
light and darkness.
Thus sorrow and joy
pervade our lives.
Hands being folded tell us:
there are two poles of reality.
We profess the polarity of our existence.

In folding our hands we point them
upward to God.

There is more to life than just the world,
my worries, my problems, things that depress.
I lift myself up.
I lift up my heart to God
the same way I lift up my hands.
They are like two towers,
like two church steeples that point to on high.
They point to God.
No matter what happens—God is present.
No matter what happens—
God is my help.
I fold my hands, say nothing at first.
Take a while to quiet down.
Lay one finger over the other—
this relieves tension.
I enter that quiet room
of which Jesus spoke:
"When you pray, enter your room!"
The room is peace, it is quiet.
Quiet must come before all else!
In the quiet the Lord draws near to us.

The opposite of folded hands is
the clenched fist.
Many who are unable to pray, clench their fists.

Nothing can enter
or exit a fist.
The fist symbolizes isolation,
embitterment, and seclusion.
Those who do not pray are in jeopardy of
isolating themselves,
making permanent their embitterment.
They think they are entitled
to their bitterness.
Those who clench their fists are no longer capable
of receiving,
they live in a state of denial, of death.
Therefore, it is essential for people
who are bitter,
who clench their fists,
to pray.
If I hope for a person,
believe for a person,
pray for a person,
then their clench can be loosened,
and through my hope
that person can be resurrected.

OUTSTRETCHED ARMS

My arms are outstretched.
I am ready to receive.
I am ready to embrace.
I praise you!
I rejoice
that You are, O God!
I come to You!
You are there.
I embrace You.
I give You my hand!
I rejoice!

I need You!
Here are my hands.
Hold me!
Hold me,
save me!
I am sinking.
Jesus, You pulled Peter up out of the water
when he began to doubt.
Here are my hands!
I too am sinking.
Hold me!

STANDING

Standing upright,
standing still.
Listening.
I am ready.
I am ready,
I collect myself.
I am here!
Standing.
Standing here, still, thoughts collected,
to be filled by God's thoughts,
and to be reached by His grace,
by His peace.
Standing here, ready
to accept an assignment.
Standing here as a sign of readiness:
I am here!

WALKING

The path of a procession—a pilgrimage.
I walk.
Follow the path.
Think about the path my life has taken.
Step by step—
I cannot leap over anything.
Everything needs time.
I need hours to arrive at a destination.
Walking.
Not sitting, not standing around, walking!
Moving on.
Not standing around a thought
and growing stiff.
Not standing around a word or a letter
and getting stuck.
Not becoming impassive: walking, moving!
Turning always anew to various sights,
always anew to people.
Walking!
Walking to God,
sitting before God,
standing before God,
kneeling before God,
lying down before God.

Everything releases something within us!
Thus, it is important
to set aside time
for these various postures.
Only then can that which is external
permeate to our innermost core.

SITTING

Sitting here—
concentrating.
Sitting still.
Just being here.
Not wanting anything,
just listening, listening attentively.
Letting the many voices within me
grow quiet.
Sitting here—
growing silent.
If I change the way I sit,
I grow quiet again.
This creates a climate
in which a word read to me
can move me.
I need a setting,
I need an atmosphere of trust
in order for God's word to take hold of me.
Sitting here—
and being still!
The posture of trust,
the posture of receptivitiy.

KNEELING

We all want to succeed,
to be hard-working, to accomplish something,
to be recognized, to be honored.
We want to be somebody;
above all, we want to be greater than others.
We consider ourselves smarter
than others.
We also consider ourselves better
than others.
Kneeling is an act of humility.
I give public witness that
I acknowledge a Lord who is over me;
I acknowledge an absolute spirit
whom I allow to inspire me;
I acknowledge a Lord who leads me;
I acknowledge a plan which is greater
than my plan,
a will, that is stronger than my will.
I kneel. I worship.
I bow down before God and in doing so say:
"Speak! Your servant is listening.
Lead! Lead me!
I want to follow You!
Show me Your will,
I will do it!
It is not I who am the center of the world,

You are!
It is not I who created the world,
You did!"
I kneel.

PRAYER (KNEELING)

I bow down in worship before You,
great God.
I bown down in worship
before the being,
before the soul,
before the ego
that you have placed within me
and that extends beyond me.
You are rooted in me
and I revere You
within me.
I kneel before You
because of the beautiful feeling
that there is something infinitely great,
greater than I can imagine,
too powerful for me to fathom,
too vast for me to grasp.
I thank You!

DIRECTIONS FOR SEEKERS:

Meditations on the Basic Truths of Christianity

THE FIRST BASIC TRUTH

There is a God

I look . . . I'm standing by my window at night and looking out. A universe, full of stars. Every star as powerful and large as our sun. Only a tiny number can be seen with the naked eye.

Millions of stars. Millions of light years away, a superabundance of energy! For billions of years they have radiated light.

That's when I think of God.

I'm standing in the pediatrics ward, peering through a window into a room of newborn babies. Twenty little lives before my eyes—human children, human fates! What will these humans grow up to be? Ten, twenty, forty, sixty, ninety years old! What will they look like? What will they be when they leave this world? Mature, bitter, humble?

That's when I ask God questions!

I enter a church. The noise within me has quieted down. I hear nothing. I wait a while. I arrive at the entrance to my own self. I find myself. Statues of the saints stand before me. They are at peace. They are complete.

I am in the midst of battle. After a while I sigh "O God," make the Sign of the Cross, and commingle once again among people who hate and who love.

Who is God—Who am I? To answer this question, I would first have to deal with the question "Who am I?" But no matter how persistently I put this question to psychologists, doctors, and philosophers, they cannot provide a good or clear enough explanation of who I am. I remain a puzzle, a mystery to myself.

Before any experience of God must come the experience of oneself. Many of our contemporaries have lost true contact with themselves. They wage war against themselves. Most of the time they run away from great experiences like sorrow, regret, love, joy. They try to live a plain, ordinary, uneventful life. Is this how they will find God? God is found not only in the heavens and beyond the heavens. God is found in people. How can people always on the run from themselves come to God? They will flee to an image of God from their childhood, they will pray to an imaginary God, to a dream image. That dream image prevents them from really confronting themselves. The result for many is a breakdown, because their image of God has been frozen in time.

What is your image of God? It says for good reason in the Old Testament: "Do not make for yourselves any idols" (Exodus 20:4).

We humans think in images. The images we invent are not dangerous, but clinging to them is. Only few people progress in the way they think. What they once heard about God many years ago, they never related to their own life's experiences. They remain stuck at the developmental level of a grade schooler.

It is essential that we continue to grow in knowledge and faith until our imminent encounter with God in death.

Countless people have become spiritually ill, because their dream images remained frozen in time. God is how HE is, and not how we were taught, or how we want Him to be. All we can do is encounter Him daily, enter into a new relationship with Him daily, listen to Him daily.

In prayer, silence is more important than speaking. "As long as we talk, God must remain silent," says the great Christian mystic, Johannes Tauler.

Don't worry and fret, just pray! Rarely does God reveal Himself to those who worry and fret. God surrenders Himself to those who pray and stand in awe of Him. After an exciting life in the pharaoh's palace, Moses withdrew into the desert. He lived in hiding. He had time to observe and to marvel. It was during this time that God met him in the burning bush. God introduces Himself to Moses with the unusual words: "I AM WHO AM" (Exodus 3:14). Moses pressed God to reveal His name and other important characteristics, because the Israelites wanted an exact description of God's person. God does not agree to a more detailed revelation. He reveals Himself and conceals Himself. He says: "I am here just for you." He can only be experienced in an encounter. In his drama *The Count of Ratzeburg,* Ernst Barlach confesses: "I have no God, but God has me."

God is Love. Sacred Scripture makes many statements about God. All the references coalesce in a vision provided by Saint John, who says: "God is love" (1 John 4:8). Every other profession of faith is subordinate to this basic truth.

Saint Augustine says that because God is good (i.e., loving), we exist. The Christian apologist Boethius acknowledges that it is God's nature to empty Himself and to share. Creation is a result of God's longing to share. Because God is love, people who love can experience much of God's nature. Those who immerse themselves in the mystery of God as love will have fear, doubt, cowardice, bitterness taken from them. We should rejoice in God.

God is for us, not against us. God is within us every second, no matter where we are, no matter who we are. God is loyal. His nature is one of love, not revenge. Our own lives will be radically transformed if we can believe in a God of love.

You yourselves must be moved. (The following has been adapted from Antoine de Saint-Exupéry.) If you do not modify your behavior in love toward a new face that reveals itself to you (and in you establishes a new love), and if you instead allow yourself to be moved by a mild breeze that carries with it only a fruitless logic and is without substance, then I will disown you.

Because people do not die for a sign, but for the pledge which underlies the sign. And if you should want to express the latter, you would require more knowledge than is contained in all the books of the world. Because what I have so obtained, I will not let you give away. You yourselves must be moved in order that you might absorb the entire meaning of the mountain that my poem contains.

How many words would I have to use if I wanted you to experience a mountain and you had never left the ocean?

The same can be said of a fountain. If you never thirst, and if you have never pressed both your hands together to reach out and catch water, then you will never know what refreshment awaits you. Of course, I can sing the praises of a fountain, but what about the experience, and what about the muscles that will awaken the memory within you?

And so, if I wish to teach you about God, I will first let you go mountain climbing, that you might come to know what a steep slope in full majesty under the stars is. I will let you die of thirst in the desert.

The limits of language and expression. God cannot be compressed into any creed. He cannot really be described. Everything we say about Him amounts to little more than hints and allusions. For this reason doctrines about God are approximations, never definitive conclusions. Our thoughts and descriptions of God should never become fixed. A fixed image of God turns into an idol. Thus, whoever would praise God will need to be watchful and alert. This is why we hear the Bible repeat the charge: "Watch and pray!" In other words, live in such a way that God can encounter you! Whenever God was made comprehensible, people took away His power to attract. Too much confident talk about God is a sign that the ability to be moved is lacking.

God presents Himself to us. That is the deepest meaning of the word *present*. That is why we are only able to encounter God "now [i.e., in the present] or never."

For Private Reflection

All statements about God are incomplete allusions that must be completed and deepened through our prayer.

It is not we who have God, but God who has us.

In order to encounter God, we must be collected, seek silence, and meditate.

God is love. This love extends far beyond any human capacity to understand love.

We should not create dream images of God. Rather, we should constantly examine our life experiences, allowing our faith to grow and develop daily. God created us out of love for us.

God remains loyal to us. He does not withdraw His hand and abandon us as husband, wife, children, and friends might.

God is at our side for eternity.

Bible Passages for Meditation

"I will be with you; I will be your God and you will be my people" (Leviticus 26:12).

"God is not like human beings" (Numbers 23:19).

"No one has ever seen God" (John 1:18).

"Everyone will be taught by God" (John 6:45).

THE SECOND BASIC TRUTH

In God are three Persons: Father, Son, and Holy Spirit

I stand atop a mountain. I am surrounded by majestic mountain peaks. A view so beautiful, it makes me wish it would last forever! Peaks and valleys. Dreams turned into mountains. A paradise. I thank God, my Father and Creator.

I search for a way within. I torment myself with questions. I read books. They do not help me grow. Suddenly, I meet a wise, old man. He listens intently to me. He responds and becomes a source of inspiration. He strengthens that which is positive within me. At the same time he criticizes and encourages me. I am moved. I sense clearly God's presence before me. God has spoken to me. God in the guise of a seventy-year-old man.

I sit in my room. I am listening to a Beethoven symphony on the radio. I give the music my complete attention. After a while I find myself filled by the power and dynamism of the music. From within I am transformed into a single hymn of praise. I feel God within me.

Jesus speaks of the Father and of the Holy Spirit. Jesus provides His apostles with a living example of unity with the Father. "I am the true vine, and my Father is the grower" (John 15:1). Jesus is certain of His unity with the Father. Jesus promises His apostles that He will come with the Father. "Whoever keeps my commandments, loves me; whoever loves me is loved by the Father, and I will love him and reveal myself to him" (John 14:21). "As the Father has loved me, so I have loved you. Remain steadfast in your love for one another" (John 15:9). Jesus promises to send the Holy Spirit, the indwelling and eternal Paraclete: "If you love me, you will keep my commandments. And I will ask the Father, and He will give you a new helper who will remain with you forever. It is the Spirit of Truth, whom the world cannot receive because it does not see It or know It. But you will know It because It will remain with you and abide in you" (John 14:15–17).

God above us, God with us, God in us. The Bible clearly shows us that God does not view human struggles dispassionately or without empathy from His heavenly throne. He participates in our history. God comes down from heaven. He draws close to us humans. In

Jesus of Nazareth God Himself becomes human. God does not just offer help from a safe distance. In Jesus Christ He wants to understand us as human beings, to help us, heal us, and redeem us. God extends Himself. He becomes human and remains God. He becomes vulnerable and weary, yet remains all-powerful.

Safeguard against error. The doctrine of the Holy Trinity can help prevent us from making God into a distant, incomprehensible spirit. On the other hand, the doctrine can guard us against seeing Jesus as nothing more than a good person who was a failure. It counters any misunderstanding that the Holy Spirit gives validity to our institutions, or that the Holy Spirit is to be equated with revolutionary activities or a wealth of ideas on our part. What the doctrine of the Trinity tells us is God is closer to us than we think. Jesus is more demanding than we care to admit. The Church is more than the sum of all its offices.

God is everywhere. The doctrine of the Most Holy Trinity shows God's involvement with human beings. God does not just create the world and then abandon it to the forces of good and evil. God did not withdraw from the world following His work of salvation. God is ever-present. He suffers, dies, and is risen. God does not abandon human beings. He does not just accompany them as a guide. Rather, He becomes an inner voice, an inner counselor within every human. The doctrine of the Holy Spirit can make us aware of the manifold presence of God: God in heaven, God on earth, God above, God below, God over us, God beneath us, God with us, God in us. Anyone who attempts to comprehend the existence of God strictly through logic is like a person who tries to empty the ocean with a spoon. The basic thing about God is that He is unlimited, unparalleled, and incomprehensible. God is more than a judge with notebook in hand, waiting to enter plus and minus points.

God is more than a person who dies a lonely death on the cross. God is not only eternal and unborn. In Jesus He enters the world as a mortal. He grows, He develops, and He matures.

The Incomprehensible One. The doctrine of the Trinity touches on the incomprehensibility of God. Some people would like to try and make God comprehensible. They would like to reduce this teaching to a few comprehensible sentences. When they do, they deprive people of substantive opportunities for growth and development. Because the smaller and more comprehensible God becomes, the poorer it is that people will remain. They would like to scale God down to their size. But in so doing, they make God into an idol. In every age we will have to grapple with the incomprehensibility of God. He will never be able to be understood or depicted in His entirety. We will never be able to form a complete image of Him. Who will ever be able to understand how God can be all-powerful (God as Creator) as well as powerless (God on the cross), or that He can be infinitely distant (God in heaven) as well as infinitely close (God in us), or that God can be simultaneously brother and judge? If we really want to experience God, it is necessary that we gather new life experiences on a daily basis. We can experience the way God works in our everyday lives. That is how we will be able to move closer to God. Through our life experiences we will receive answers appropriate for many of our questions.

For Private Reflection

People can experience God in a variety of ways: as Lord and Creator, as Father of all, as brother and guide, as counselor, as advocate, and as One who always helps.

God's experiences with people are portrayed in the Bible. The teaching of the Trinity evolves from biblical testimony. People have meditated on experiences they have had with God.

God is without limitations. We cannot dictate to Him how He is supposed to act. He encounters us as God and man, in the world within and the world without. He encounters us as the Suffering One, the One who failed (in Jesus), and as the Almighty. The teaching of the Trinity challenges our thinking and our faith. We cannot say that God is *only* Father, *only* brother, or *only* counselor. He is all things and all things completely. Every person will experience God differently. We must be humble in our thoughts. We will never be able to comprehend the complete truth, because God and His works are greater than we can ever be.

Bible Passages for Meditation

"In him we live and move and have our being, as some of your poets have said: 'We too are his children'" (Acts 17:28).

"We know that in all things God works for good with those who love him" (Romans 8:28).

"If God is for us, who can be against us?" (Romans 8:31).

"But you belong to Christ, and Christ belongs to God" (1 Corinthians 3:23).

THE THIRD BASIC TRUTH

The Son of God became man to redeem us through His death on the cross and to bring us eternal life

A magnificent summer day. I'm out taking a long walk. I pass by many crosses. I stop at one. My eyes fall on the face of Him crucified. A strange surrender in pain! That face—I cannot get it out of my mind. I start to think: who is He, from whom Christianity springs forth? A deep thinker? A dreamer? A failed idealist? Has He finally died? Is He more than just a pious legend? What have we Christians revealed to the world about Jesus? Is He just a man or the Son of God? What did He really think? What did He feel? How did He deal with His fears, His desires, His questions and doubts? Did He die full of hope? Full of despair? Are the Gospel accounts accurate, or have they been colored by people's awe and admiration?

Who is this man, who had such a profound influence on the way hundreds of thousands of people think, act, and behave?

Our image of Jesus. Some people have a cliché-like image of Jesus that they have carried with them since childhood and never questioned. They see Him as the guarantor of peace, consolation, and comfort. Others admire Him as the great social critic who endeavored to shake the establishment. Still others see Him as a harmless idealist who became a victim of reality. Just one more person who was unable to deal with the evil of this world. Some people meditate at length on who He was. Others just regurgitate opinions they have come to adopt as their own.

There is no shortage of theologies, interpretations, images, and experiences of Jesus Christ. It is true that the Gospels contain the message of Jesus, but the evangelists speak of Him only indirectly as a person. There is no officially approved book on Christ. Based on the gospel accounts, Jesus must have had a multifaceted personality. His mind was as sharp as a razor, but there was also an intense emotional side to Him. Even the best educated scribes could not entrap Him. Most of what Jesus said was symbolic. He did not approach people with rules, but told parables and stories. These parables can be interpreted in a number of different ways. He also managed to survive the greatest of split personalities. He is "true God" and "true man." Jesus said: "Be as cunning as snakes and as naivé as doves!" He loved His apostles. "I do not call you servants, but friends." And yet He called Peter "Satan" when Peter tried to get Him to walk a different path. He spoke as one with authority, yet remained silent before Pilate.

No biased thinking. Jesus approves of tax monies going to Caesar. At the same time He points to the necessity of surrender to God. He challenges His apostles: "Do not worry about your lives and what you will eat, nor about your bodies or what you have to wear." On the other hand, He says in the parable about the talents that people should concentrate on their own individual talents. He demands an all-out effort. Church history shows how oftentimes people have forced certain words of Jesus into the limelight, while remaining silent over others. This has caused injury to no small number of Christians. Our focus must be on Christ *in His entirety.* Jesus came to liberate people from their small-minded way of thinking, blind obedience to laws, and narrow-minded faith. He shows us an attitude toward life that liberates and strengthens.

Jesus challenges us to conversion. Jesus asks questions that get at the heart of why people are living and thinking the way they are. In so doing, He becomes a source of irritation. But He is motivated from deep within: "The Father and I are one." The nature of His being derives from unity with the Father. This unity makes it possible for Him to perform miracles. In Jesus' death His close relationship with the Father becomes obvious. According to Mark's account, Jesus dies with the words: "My God, my God, why have you forsaken me?" In Luke, the last words of Jesus are: "Father, into your hands I commend my spirit."

Jesus' entire gospel message reveals His intimate relationship with the Father. It challenges us to contemplation and conversion. "The time is come, the kingdom of God is near. Repent and believe in the gospel!"

Jesus sets us free. Jesus teaches as one with authority, and not like the scribes. He appears on the scene as a wise Jewish teacher. He teaches in the synagogue and debates with opponents. People ask Jesus questions, for example, about the meaning and application of the commandments. His answers to those questions are unusual. He quickly gains recognition among the people as an authority in scriptural interpretation and is thus addressed with the title *rabbi* (master, teacher). But Jesus quickly proves Himself to be different from the other rabbis of his day. He does so through the directness of His parables and through the freedom with which He interprets Old Testament laws. He synthesizes the hundred or so various laws into the basic commandment to love God, self, and neighbor. People must not be satisfied with mere formal fulfillment of the law. They must look after their neighbor. "The Sabbath was created for man, not man for the Sabbath."

Loving. The unity of love toward God and neighbor becomes manifest in Jesus Himself. He is completely one with the Father. At the same time, He exists completely for us. The same Jesus who helps so many people, repeatedly retreats from people in order to be alone with the Father and to pray (cf. Matthew 14:23; Mark 1:35 and 6:46; Luke 6:12 and 9:28).

Rethinking. "The time is come, the kingdom of God is near. Repent and believe in the Gospel!" Viewed from a historical perspective, the reality of Jesus occurs during a period of many expectations. Jesus speaks forcefully and simply of the Kingdom of God. God reveals Himself. The prophets also testified to this. Jesus goes even further: He proclaims: "The time is come!" Now God reveals Himself through Jesus.

Jesus—our brother. "The Son of Man did not come to be served, but to serve, to give Himself as a ransom for many." Jesus' authority comes from His example. He lives what He says. He is loyal and generous, He sacrifices and forgives. Particularly in His encounters with women and children and with the outcasts of society, Jesus shows Himself to be a person who is there for others. The Pharisees and scribes are shocked by this and say: "He associates with sinners and even eats with them." Jesus hears that and says: "It is not the healthy who need a doctor, but the sick. I have come to call sinners, not the righteous."

Jesus heals. Jesus did things that deepened people's impression of his authority. Most of Jesus' miracles were cures. They represent an unequivocal affirmation of life and a rejection of sickness and death.

Jesus does not want admirers, but followers! "Not everyone who says to me: Lord! Lord! will enter the kingdom of heaven, but only those who have done the will of my Father." To His apostles Jesus says: "Whoever would follow me must first deny himself, then pick up his cross and follow me." It was customary among the Jews of that time for highly esteemed teachers of the law to recruit a number of students so that their teachings might be passed on. What immediately sets Jesus' students apart, however, is that they did not belong to the upper echelons of society. For the most part, they were simple fishermen from Galilee, a small strip of land in the country that was viewed with contempt. Jesus demanded much from His disciples. He did not want a temporary working arrangement, but a life-long commitment to a way of living, suffering, and discipleship. Often Jesus' disciples did not understand Him. They quickly lost courage and abandoned Him in the critical hours of His suffering. Judas betrayed Him. Peter denied Him. Both were apostles expressly chosen by Jesus.

Jesus suffers. Jesus did not die as one honored by religious or civic leaders, but as one condemned. One of the most moving experiences Christians can have is when they are in a crisis and look at Him crucified, and He awakens in them hope and confidence.

Jesus Christ is risen from the dead. The New Testament was written from the conviction that the Lord did not remain dead; He was truly risen! With the Resurrection of Jesus it is not only His story that continues. Jesus continues to meet His apostles. He converses and eats with them. He allows them to touch Him. There is some talk of doubt among the apostles. Various reports speak of trembling and fear. But the apostles are told: "Do not be afraid! You seek Jesus of Nazareth, the One crucified. He is risen; He is not here. Look, there is the place where they laid Him." The realization of what Easter means did not become apparent to the apostles until after the appearance of the Risen Christ (disciples on the road to Emmaus).

Jesus, the Way, the Truth, and the Life. "And whoever lives and believes in me will have life eternal. Do you believe that?" Jesus came in order to endow people with a worldview full of hope. He informed us of a truth that gives lasting meaning to people of all ages. A person is a son or daughter of God, a child of God. God goes out to meet his lost son and gives a feast. Jesus embraces life to the fullest. He liberates people from sickness, prejudices, and narrow-minded thinking. He is a witness to the reality of God in this time, in this world.

For Private Reflection

The Gospels are first and foremost eyewitness accounts of early Christian beliefs in Jesus.

Jesus did not appear on the scene as a political freedom fighter, but rather as a preacher of God's all-embracing renewal of humankind. He proclaims the kingdom of God.

Jesus should not be seen in a mono-dimensional way. He was neither a social revolutionary nor a preacher out of touch with the world.

Jesus attaches equal importance to love of God and love of neighbor. He comes to the defense of outcasts. However, He also accepts invitations from those in high society.

Jesus places extremely high expectations on people. Whoever wants to follow Him must put aside all else, including marriage, family, and worldly possessions.

Jesus came as the master teacher of life. He wanted to show people how they could give meaning to their lives.

Jesus was at the complete service of God and man. He listened to the Father and obeyed. From unity with the Father He derived strength to heal the sick and raise the dead.

Jesus gathered His disciples around Him. He confided in them everything He knew about the Father. Jesus lived in community with His disciples. It was in this community of disciples that the church was conceived.

Jesus fell into disfavor with leading figures of the Jewish community because of His sharp criticism of the Pharisees. They had Him arrested. They tried Him. He was sentenced to death.

Jesus is God and man. He is the crucified and risen Lord. As the risen and transfigured Lord He remains always near to us. With us He will conquer history and write its final chapter.

Bible Passages for Meditation

"Repent. The Kingdom of God is near" (Matthew 4:17).

"I praise you, Father, Lord of heaven, because all that you have hidden from the clever and wise, you have revealed to the merest of children" (Luke 10:21).

"At the cross of Jesus stood His mother, His sister's mother, Mary, the wife of Clopas, and Mary Magdalene" (John 19:25).

"He who gives this testimony says: 'Yes, I am coming soon.' Amen. Come, Lord Jesus!" (Revelation 20:22).

THE FOURTH BASIC TRUTH

God is a righteous judge who rewards the good and punishes the wicked

I have this feeling in the morning . . . Nothing is going right. My anger mounts. I snarl at co-workers. I scream into the phone. I'd give anything just to blast someone. Somebody says to me: What's wrong? What's with you? Why don't you go take a fifteen-minute break! Try and get yourself together! Then come on back to the office! I take the advice. During the quiet time questions surface: What put me into such a foul mood? What is making me so angry? What have I become over the past few weeks and months? Unbearable? There's no reason for me to be acting this way. I'm healthy and have lots of friends. I'm very hard on myself. Everything should be happening even more quickly than it already is. I want to be even more successful. I want to be able to buy myself even more things, and so on. All these things get me worked up. Isn't it more important to lead a balanced life and to radiate warmth to people already stressed? There are enough angry people around. But people who can hear are in danger of extinction. I can change myself. The power to do so lies within me. I can become a human being or a monster. After a short while, my inner peace has returned. I can feel how my anger abates. Newfound vigor returns. I treat my co-workers friendlier than before. Suddenly my surroundings seem friendlier. I have become different.

What counts. The Sermon on the Mount centers on radical compliance to God's will. Jesus' message must not be reduced to a compilation of laws. Will God be satisfied with obedience grounded in fear and strict adherence to the letter of the law? Isn't there more than "Thou shalts" and "Thou shalt nots"? That would be omitting one thing that does have quite an impact on human behavior. God wants more! He demands more than a half-hearted effort. He demands total commitment. He requires not only exterior manifestations of my conversion, which I can easily control for effect, but He requires an interior conversion of the heart—something I cannot control. He desires not only good fruit, but a good tree. Not only my deeds, but my very being. Not just anything, but me myself. The Sermon on the Mount is not to be understood as law. Jesus is not a lawyer. He appeals, He clarifies, but He issues no legal statutes.

Be good or something more? Why didn't Jesus leave behind a clear list of rules and regulations? Jesus obligates His apostles with the words: "Be perfect, even as your heavenly Father is perfect." He prays: "Your will be done!" In the Acts of the Apostles, Peter and John defend themselves before the Sanhedrin with the argument that the law may distract people from meditating and hearing the will of God. Most people do not make a daily effort to discern anew God's will. Consequently, they make the wrong decisions over and over again. Granted, observation of their actions may lead one to conclude that they are fulfilling the requirements of the law, but deep within they are unhappy nonetheless. People must attune themselves to God's will daily. Those who limit themselves to keeping God's law could be thinking that if they simply keep the law, God will be satisfied. But there is far more to it than that. And so, it is only in daily prayer that I can discern God's will. This requires time. But a daily encounter with God is the only way we can know God's thoughts. When our will and God's are in agreement, I will experience peace.

Jesus—Our Way. "Repent and believe in the Gospel!" Jesus is not only the truth. He is also the way. We should think like Jesus does about enemies, outcasts, the self-righteous, etc. Our standard must be the imitation of Jesus. Jesus talks not only of challenges. He begins His discourses with promises; for example, "You are the salt of the earth . . . you are the light of the world. A city located atop a mountain cannot remain hidden."

What Jesus demands. Every person is called to grow beyond their ordinary, everyday thoughts, and beyond negative emotions like anger, hatred, jealousy. Without daily meditation we will not reach maturity. People must come to know who they are. Most of the time we deceive ourselves. Through relentless self-examination, we can unmask those deceptions. There are not just a few so-called "decent" people who are basically just hypocrites. They deceive themselves. They still lack the courage to examine themselves in-depth. They flee moments of quiet. It is the quiet that poses us questions from which we cannot escape. But some people remain greedy, dissatisfied, overly busy, unmoved, and totally oblivious until their dying day. Not until purgatory will they come to a true realization of who they are. Purgatory will be that stage of development where we will be able to "catch up" and "grow to full maturity."

Our conscience. Our conscience is much like a compass or radar that signals us of impending danger. Before an act it spurs us on or warns us. After our decision it may react with discomfort or with satisfaction. No one can take away our decisions of conscience—not the church, not the Pope. A person's conscience is grounded in their freedom. In today's world, the individual's decisions of conscience are taking on ever-greater importance. Through the growth of technical and scientific possibilities, people's responsibilities have become broader. Our conscience is always in danger of meekly succumbing and surrendering to that which is personally advantageous. Pride, the spirit of the times, passion, and ego can corrupt and distort the judgment of one's conscience for personal gains. Just as any measurement device must be examined in order to determine whether it provides accurate readings, our conscience must be calibrated against the commandments. Jesus says: "Those who follow me will not walk in darkness [aimlessly]."

People reward and punish themselves. Many people fear God because they only see Him as Judge. But God is not a judge who acts in an arbitrary manner. He makes no exceptions. He is impartial. God has established the laws of nature, of our soul, and of the universe. "People reap what they have sown."

God does not judge. People judge themselves. Those who do not believe have already been judged. Every evil act has consequences. People who are jealous, vengeful, and greedy will bring about their own destruction. They may prevail for a while. But one day they will realize the emptiness and loneliness in their lives. That will be their judgment. People who grow accustomed to half-truths and lies will have no confidence or trust in others. They will be destroyed by the imaginary world construed by their lies. People who worry only about themselves and who have no respect for others will find that when they face hopeless situations they will have no friends. People who believe they can do without God will one day have to struggle with the lack of meaning in their lives. No one need seek revenge. No one need envy another. We carry judgment within us. The facades of riches, power, and prestige tell us little about the interior disposition of a person. No one can escape her- or himself. How many people like that begin to drink! They want to forget. They want to run from themselves. People must face up to who they are, no matter what they have become. Only those who have been brutally honest with themselves can attain inner peace. Heaven, hell, and purgatory begin while we are still here on earth. We can be certain that goodness, understanding, and a willingness to help others will already bear good fruit here on earth. God gives us time to mature on earth. God has called us to give our maximum effort, not our minimum effort. "To all who are victorious, I will give to eat of the tree of life."

For Private Reflection

The message of Jesus demands that we take seriously the will of God.

Through constant discernment we can learn the will of God.

People are called to perfection.

People judge and punish themselves. No person can escape her- or himself.

Superficial obedience to God's laws will not suffice for the development of one's full human potential.

Attitude is important in this regard, as are clarity of thought and human sincerity. Jesus uses sharp words to denounce the self-righteousness, hypocrisy, and deceit of the Pharisees.

Jesus does not deny the existence of sin and judgment. He forgives and helps people make a fresh start.

Heaven, hell, and purgatory have already begun here on earth; this will be plain for all to see in eternity.

Bible Passages for Meditation

"I know, my God, that you examine all hearts" (1 Chronicles 29:17).

"Learn to do good! Do what is right! Help the oppressed! Give orphans their rights, protect those who are widowed!" (Isaiah 1:17).

"Good deeds are like trees that bear marvelous fruit, and like roots from which new shoots always shoot up" (Wisdom 3:15).

"If you love me, you will keep my commands" (John 14:15).

"Do not let evil defeat you; rather, conquer evil with good" (Romans 12:21).

"Fight the good fight of faith, win for yourself the eternal life to which you have been called, and for which you have professed your faith before many witnesses" (1 Timothy 6:12).

THE FIFTH BASIC TRUTH

Without God's grace we cannot become holy

Grace and human accomplishment. A man turns to me for help. He is despairing. His wife is having an affair with his friend. He wants to end his life. I sit across from a destroyed man. At first I struggle to control my own emotions. What should I say? What should I do? Then I begin to calm down. I try to be there completely for him. I try to concentrate on this fellow human being sitting across from me. In this way God will be able to speak and work in me. After a while he says: "I can't hate anymore." He has received the courage to continue on with his life.

Who, in a conversation of that sort, could possibly separate with any degree of preciseness the human involvement from the divine? To what extent was *I* able to help that person? And to what extent did God influence him through what I had to say, through my quiet listening? How much was due to grace, how much was due to human accomplishment?

Jesus and the adulteress. They brought an adulteress to Jesus. The law of Moses demanded that such a person be stoned. Jesus said to her self-righteous accusers: "Let the one among you who is without sin cast the first stone!" After a period of silence, Jesus turned to the woman and asked her if there was anyone left to accuse her. She answered: "There is no one, Lord!" Then Jesus said: "Then neither will I condemn you. Go and sin no more!" Here forgiveness was granted without it even being requested. Here forgiveness of sin takes place without confession. Under any human system of law, this would have been an impossibility. But it is God's way.

God's charm. The apostles searched for a word that could express the forgiving love of Jesus. Accordingly, they selected the Greek word *charis,* which we sometimes translate as "grace." Unfortunately, this word has become so overused in theological discussions that nowadays we might be better off to speak of goodness and compassion when expressing God's basic nature.

God longs for us. We are loved. God created us. He rejoices in our development. He wants life and happiness for us. He rejoices over our growth. God finds us attractive. Thus, we should not wear ourselves out through constant self-reproach. If God likes us, we too should love ourselves. Many people wear themselves out from negative thinking. God did not create us so that we would loathe ourselves.

God's fondness for us. Everyday we should say to ourselves: God likes us, God stands by us. If God is on my side, what misfortune can possibly befall me? Jesus told us that we are children of God. So why be afraid? Why moan and groan about how poor we are? We should not become enamored of our poverty. We will derive much joy from beholding God's greatness and from experiencing His divine favor. God became human in order that He might show us His heavenly favor.

Love experienced has a strengthening effect. Jesus did not only reveal Himself to those who were deserving. He also gave Himself completely to sinners and outcasts. We can count on God's generous love in whatever situation, even in times of most grievous sin. Those who have experienced grace will be able to pass it on to others. Love that has been experienced has a strengthening effect. Some of the Nazi-era resistance fighters who had been sentenced to death wrote to their parents from jail that they could die without hating their executioners and judges. And they report that they received an exceptional outpouring of love from their parents. We will never be able to help a person through hate, rejection, and criticism who is without love.

God woos us. He does not threaten us. He lets us feel His love. The love we experience from Him makes us so strong that we can even forgive our enemies.

Human beings are not inert. Human beings evolve, they become, they grow, they waste away, they become rejuvenated, they experience loneliness, they feel secure, they mature, they regress to a primitive stage, they pick themselves up again, they suffer, they think, they ponder, they regret, they change, they become attuned to their inner being, they grow calm. These stages of individual development reflect the ebb and flow of human existence—until ultimately peace is found through trust in God. God accompanies people on their human journey. Even in situations where people experience nothing but anger, hate and despair, God is able to work on the creation of a kind and patient person. It was God who loved us first. And therein lies the mystery of grace. It is not we who possess God, life, and the world—God created us. This favor, which rushed ahead without receiving human love in return, reveals to us the essence of grace. Sacred Scripture speaks of God's indomitable love for us: "I have loved you with an everlasting love, thus have I remained faithful to you for so long!"

Everything will be fine. We know that for those who love God, for those who are with God, and for those who have been called according to His eternal plan, God will bring all things to a good end.

What conclusions can we draw if we meditate thereon? If God is for us, who can be against us?

Grace enjoys a particularly close relationship with the concepts of *power* and *apostolate.* Grace is God's power to attract. Just as we are drawn to a person who is empowering, charming, and positively disposed toward us, we are drawn to God. His love for the world, humanity, and the universe is total. When I move from superficiality to intimacy, I will experience in a very special way the loving personality of God and of humanity. "This hope does not destroy us, because the love of God has been poured out into our hearts by the Holy Spirit, who has been given to us." We are surrounded by a benevolent God. Knowing that we are loved by a sublime, eternal, infinite God gives us the power to move mountains. It is said of Saint Stephen, who was one of the first martyrs to die for Christ: "But Stephen, full of grace and power, performed miracles and wondrous signs among the people."

My grace is enough for you. In the quiet recesses of his heart, the apostle Paul received this answer to his urgent prayer: "My grace is enough for you, because its power is revealed in your weakness. Therefore, I boast of my weaknesses in order that the power of Christ might come upon me."

Grace is not a gift that can be separated from the giver. Grace means God is at work. Whoever loves someone will do something for the beloved, will talk with them, caress them, lavish them with gifts. All these things come from a single source: love. Thus, grace is not a gift or force distinct from God.

God Himself is grace for humankind. Jesus reveals to us the extent of God's love through His unequivocal and deep sacrifice for His apostles, for sinners, for all people. Whenever the law and righteousness become the primary focus of attention, love will not be able to develop. It is true that everything in this world is determined by laws known and unknown; however, the source of all laws is love. This is how the gulf is bridged between law and grace.

Undeserved love. Paul writes much in his letters about grace. We do not earn God's love by our actions. We do not force Him to forgive by being good. We do not earn His favor by fearful obedience to His laws. God is not a bookkeeper or a judge who needs to always consult legal statutes. He is not a cashier who rings up our good deeds. On the contrary, God acts with charm. He offers us the gift of Himself with unpredictable generosity. In return, He hopes for a generous response. Grace is not just one in a series of things that God sends us. God Himself surrenders Himself to us. Jesus is that special charm of God. In Him we recognize God's special favor toward us. Grace, therefore, is God Himself. Because God gives Himself to us as gift. In return, He desires not just any gift, but the gift of ourselves!

Between people who love one another, there is never any bartering. Even less so between God and humans. Charm, spontaneity, generosity, and selflessness are signs of true love.

For Private Reflection

Grace is beauty, charm, goodwill, good deeds, gift, gratitude. *Grace* is another term for the love of God.

The comforting thing about the Bible's good news is that despite humanity's sin, God has not broken His covenant.

God loved us first, before we were able to do anything for Him.

God loves us even when we turn against Him.

God turns to us with unimaginable generosity and magnanimity.

God does not expect slavish adherence to His laws, rather, that we have an intimate relationship with Him.

Jesus reveals to us the charming nature of God.

People who experience grace, which is the love of God, will begin to love.

Only when people have turned to God will they find true happiness.

People who search first for the kingdom of God will experience grace upon grace.

God exists for everyone. He loves every person. Every person can count on God's favor.

The final reality of this world is not chaos, death,

hate, or judgment, but rather peace, community, forgiveness, grace, and love!

Bible Passages for Meditation

"The goodness of the Lord endures for all generations" (Psalm 103:17).

"From His fullness we have all received grace upon grace" (John 1:16).

"By God's grace I am what I am" (1 Corinthians 15:10).

"My grace is enough for you, for it reveals its strength in your weakness" (2 Corinthians 12:9).

"But the God of all grace, who has called us to His eternal glory in Christ, will Himself, after we have suffered a little while, perfect, strengthen, and establish us on a firm foundation" (1 Peter 5:10).

THE SIXTH BASIC TRUTH

The human soul is immortal

In the face of death. I have been called to the hospital. I open the door: a despaired man, despaired relatives around the bed of a dead woman. There lies a mother, not yet thirty years old, dead. I hear the words of the husband: "You can't leave yet, not now! What am I supposed to tell the children?" The eerie silence. The pale, but still-fresh face, the eyes half-opened. I am stunned. Life has retreated. We try and hold on to it! We ask: "Where are you going?" Where does a person whom we love go? Where does a person who has cared for us and done so much for us go? Where does a person go? It is only their physical remains we carry to the cemetery. Where does that person her- or himself go? I hear the words of Jesus: "I am the resurrection and the life. He who believes in me will have everlasting life . . . I go before you, to prepare a place for you . . . If a grain of wheat does not fall to the earth and die, it remains alone; but if it dies, it bears much fruit." I see people crying uncontrollably at gravesites. People who let go of a hand that has grown stiff, and who must press shut their eyes of kindness. Where do we go off to? Why suffering? Why death?

No time for questions about the end? If you stand on a street corner nowadays, you will notice how people in a city are always on the run. They are all late, hurrying. They all have to get somewhere. The minute they arrive at one destination, they rush for the next. There seems to be no end to these periodic stops. I once heard a man say to his friend: "Why is your life always so hectic? You'll die soon enough!" Death, the fact that we all must die, compels us to think about where we are headed. We have a number of intricate ways in which we avoid dealing with such questions. For one, everything that could remind us of death we banish to outside our city environs. Death is, as it were, exiled. There, on the edge of town, next to landfill sites, it is allowed to spread its fear and fright. Conversations in society about the meaning of death are dismissed with remarks like: "You're too young . . . why think about death now?"

We enter another world. We are transformed. "He is not a God of the dead, but a God of the living." Our fear of death mounts because we cling too tightly to our earthly world and devote too little time to what can be perceived beyond the senses.

Those who believe also trust. They don't just see this world, they look with their eyes and with their hearts, with finite and infinite eyes. Those who believe can already observe eternal life in this finite one. Those who believe can feel now that we Christians are temples of the Holy Spirit. Temples that cannot be destroyed. That is the meaning of the doctrine of faith that teaches that human beings have an immortal soul.

We shall live forever. Even though the oldest books of the Bible provide no exact information about immortality and our life after death, the Israelites still believed in a continuation of earthly life after death. The inescapable conclusion one draws from the uniqueness of the Creator and the uniqueness of human creation is participation in God's infinite nature. We shall live forever—it was with this song on their lips that the Jews walked into the gas chambers.

Practicing for death. In dying, a person must let go, whether they want to or not. In dying, it is the nature of our egos to offer resistance. Its whole life long the ego has always desired things for itself and sought recognition. Those who are with the dying should help them see something beyond death. Everyday we can prepare ourselves for death through the practice of letting go of something. We can free ourselves from material goods, from titles, from people, and from life. In so doing, we can become free and able to accept death without bitterness and despair as a bridge to an infinite world. Death will be overcome through profound reflection and through faith that trusts. The question posed in an Easter song: "Death, where is your victory? Death, where is your sting?" (1 Corinthians 15:55) comes to us from believers who were able to conquer at any time their fear of death by looking to Jesus Christ.

Concerning the resurrection of the dead. "This is also how it is with the resurrection of the dead. What is sown can be destroyed; what is resurrected, can never be destroyed." A person's face reveals what lies beneath. Goodness, harshness, stubbornness, a willingness to compromise, sadness, anger, and fidelity cannot be expressed without the body. The body is not just flesh and blood. It is intertwined with the Holy Spirit. We cannot separate body and soul. Only when a person is dead do they have a stiff, expressionless body. The body that was once intertwined with the Spirit is now gone, and a soulless corpse remains. A human being is immortal. When the Bible speaks of resurrection, it speaks of a person's new creation.

In Hope of the Resurrected One. The centerpiece of the New Testament's Good News is the belief in a risen Jesus. Life is more powerful than death. "Have you not read what God says about the resurrection of the dead: I am the God of Abraham, not a God of the dead, but a God of the living?" In this way Jesus points out to us quite clearly the personal relationship that this personal God has entered into with every human being. One thing is evident from the history of the people of Israel: For people who have gone astray, it means a lot to God to establish a convenant with them, to make history with them, to become friends with them. God did not call people by name to then allow them to fall into emptiness. To believe in Jesus as God is to believe in eternal life. Our belief in His power, for Whom nothing is impossible, gives us hope that we can look forward to another life rather than to death.

Resurrection of the body and soul. Jesus said to the thief on the cross: "This day, you will be with Me in paradise!"—"You" means the person, the essence of the person. The corpse remains, while the person, the you, departs. At the moment of death something comparable to the resurrection of a new body takes place. Biblical language makes no mention of human souls without bodies. Our resurrected body is not the same as the one with molecules and atoms that belongs to this earth. How this happens we do not know. It is good that we are unable to measure the magnitude of God's promise.

Resurrection on the last day. We have been created to live together, to build community. When Jesus speaks of the Last Judgment, He primarily has all of humanity in mind. The resurrection of the dead is rooted in the completion of all creation, in the transformation of the universe. From the end of the world will emerge "a new heaven and earth"—one in which the Resurrected One will destroy all the powers of evil and conquer death as the last remaining enemy (1 Corinthians 15:24–28). In this way, it is not the misery of world history that will remain, but the splendor of eternity. God will rule over all things at one and the same time. Human beings and the world were created to reach full maturity. In this faith we can apply ourselves with vigor for humankind and for the earth.

The end of the world. The goal of history is transformation, not destruction! We human beings are connected to our environment. Thus, not only will there be a resurrection of humanity, but a resurrection of all creation. In his visions John sees a new heaven and a new earth. The first heaven and the first earth have passed away. "Then I heard a loud voice from the throne cry out: Behold, the house of Lord amidst the people! He will dwell in their midst and they will be His people; and He, God, will be with them. He will wipe away every tear from their eyes. No longer will there be death, or sadness, wailing or hardship. Because what once was, has passed away" (Revelation 21:3-4).

For Private Reflection

The one thing we can all be certain of is that we must die. At all times in history people have believed in a continuation of life after death.

Human beings were created by God. God has a personal relationship with them. Because God loves human beings, He will not destroy them.

Those who learn to let go of people, goods, and accolades will die peacefully.

The core of the Christian message is belief in the Resurrection. Human beings have not been called to destruction, but to holiness.

We will be resurrected as individuals with body and soul.

In God's eyes the purpose of history is transformation, not destruction.

God, not humans, has the last word in time and in eternity.

When God leads us home, that will be a time of rejoicing!

It is not death but God that awaits us.

Bible Passages for Meditation

"You have delivered my life from death" (Psalm 56:14).

"Amen, amen, I say unto you: Whoever keeps My word will never look at death" (John 8:51).

"Death has been robbed of its victory. Death, where is your victory? Death, where is your sting?" (1 Corinthians 15:54 f.).

Whoever does not love, remains in death" (1 John 3:14).

"There will be no more death, no sadness" (Revelation 21:4).

Translator's Acknowledgments

■

Without the guidance of the Holy Spirit, this translation would never have materialized. And so my first acknowledgment goes to the Holy Spirit, source of all wisdom and comfort. Of course, Father Gutl must also be acknowledged. It was my joy to experience firsthand in the summer of 1994 that the impression Father Gutl left in person was as holy and inspirational as the one made vicariously through his publications.

Where would any artist be without the support of family and friends? To my wife, Jeanne, and to my children I am forever indebted for the sacrifices they made in order that the quality of this translation might do justice to the power and inspiration of Gutl's original work. The prayerful support and encouragement of my friends, particularly cursillistas from the dioceses of Graz, Austria and Peoria, Illinois, were also invaluable. Accordingly, I acknowledge my *Dankbarkeit* to Jane and Deacon William McClellan, David Nichols, Ed Mueller, Francis Deters, William

Richardson, Deacon Henry Hart, Mimi Krischek, Emmerich Stanz, Father Josef Jamnig, Dr. Josef Wedenig, and Father (Dr.) Herbert MeBner.

I would be remiss not to mention the Austrian Ministry of Education and Art and the University of Illinois Graduate Research Board for their support of this translation. Finally, for their guidance and steadfast encouragement, I am grateful to the Spirit-filled publishing professionals I have been privileged to work with: Father Joseph Downey, S.J., and Jeremy Langford of Loyola Press and Dr. Gerhard Trenkler of Styria Verlag in Graz.